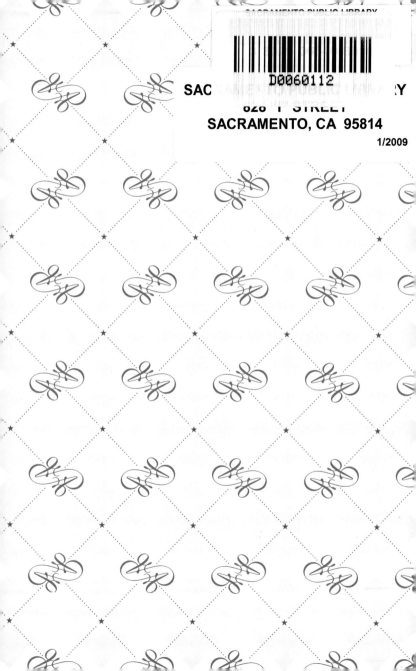

Praise for Thomas Cathcart and Daniel Klein's previous book

PLATO AND A PLATYPUS WALK INTO A BAR

Understanding Philosophy Through Jokes

"Thomas Cathcart and Daniel Klein's amusing book *Plato and a Platypus Walk Into a Bar: Understanding Philosophy Through Jokes* has been bouncing around the hardcover nonfiction list for weeks now."
THE NEW YORK TIMES

"This curious match of amusing with a musing is the true story of how Dan Klein of Great Barrington and Tom Cathcart of Sandwich conceived the zaniest bestseller of the year."
THE BOSTON GLOBE

"[V]ery funny jokes that illustrate questions and principles in metaphysics, logic, epistemology, ethics, philosophy of language, existentialism."
THE GLOBE AND MAIL (TORONTO)

"A sense of (dialectical) humor is key in life. And we all . . . need to free ourselves at times from the existential pain of our habitual existence. Why not read about Plato, Kant, and Halle Berry then? Sounds like a great legitimate distraction."
BUSINESSWEEK.COM

"You guys are good . . . Hats off to you!"
NPR, ON POINT RADIO, TOM ASHBROOK

"Consider it Philosophy 101 as taught by Jackie Mason."
HARVARD MAGAZINE

* *

ARISTOTLE

and an

AARDVARK

GO TO WASHINGTON

Understanding Political Doublespeak
Through Philosophy and Jokes

THOMAS CATHCART
&
DANIEL KLEIN

ABRAMS IMAGE, NEW YORK

* *

EDITOR: Ann Treistman
DESIGNER: Brady McNamara
PRODUCTION MANAGER: Jacquie Poirier

Parts of this book originally appeared on the Op-Ed page of *The Boston Globe*

LIBRARY OF CONGRESS CATALOGING-IN-PUBLICATION DATA

Cathcart, Thomas, 1940–
Aristotle and an aardvark go to Washington : understanding political doublespeak
through philosophy and jokes / by Thomas Cathcart and Daniel Klein.
p. cm.
ISBN-13: 978-0-8109-9541-3   ISBN-10: 0-8109-9541-7
1. United States—Politics and government—Humor. I. Klein, Daniel M. II. Title.
PN6231.P6C38 2008
401'.41—dc22
2007030690

PRINTED AND BOUND IN THE U.S.A.
10 9 8 7 6 5 4 3 2 1

HNA ▮▮▮▮▮
harry n. abrams, inc.
a subsidiary of La Martinière Groupe

115 West 18th Street
New York, NY 10011
www.hnabooks.com

To the memory of that fabulous political quipster of yore
WILL ROGERS,
who nailed it when he said,
*"There's no trick to being a humorist when you have
the whole government working for you."*

Contents
—∞—

Introduction 9

PART I: The Tricky Talk Strategy
Misleading with Doublespeak 19

PART II: The "So's Your Mother" Strategy
Misleading by Getting Personal................... 67

PART III: The Fancy Footwork Strategy
Misleading with Informal Fallacies............... 105

PART IV: The *Star Trek* Strategy
Misleading by Creating an Alternate Universe........ 131

PART V: Extra Credit
Misleading with Way Twisty Formal Fallacies 151

PART VI: The Debates
Misleading by Fabrication (Ours) 167

Pop Quiz 172
Selected Bios of Bullshitters 175
Notes 182
Illustration Credits 183
Index 185
Acknowledgments 192

—៱៱—

"That sounds like utter bullshit!"

These words spring to our minds—and occasionally our lips—just about every time we hear a politico or pundit deliver a speech or give a press conference or hold forth on some Sunday-morning talk show. But often, for the life of us, we can't figure out exactly what makes their pronouncements qualify as certifiable BS. We know in our guts they don't make sense, but we can't put our finger on why.

Certainly there are times when the politico's words fail to make sense simply because they convey a bald-faced lie. The speaker is a dissembler, a purveyor of disinformation, a fibber. As a scientist or epistemologist might delicately put it, the speaker's propositions do not correspond to the facts. But we aren't going to go there, in part because we were not permitted a sufficient number of pages to cover the most egregious political whoppers perpetrated in the last ten years (72,383, by our informal estimate). Furthermore, how many

* *

times can you shout "Liar! Liar! Pants on fire!" without getting hoarse?

Nope, we are perplexed and intrigued by subtler stuff: words that have been cunningly fashioned to sound like they mean something—something important and compelling—but that on careful inspection can be revealed to be bullshit. Often, as the senator below discovered, it's just a small step into bullshit:

It was election time again, so a senatorial candidate decided to go to the local reservation to gather support from the Native Americans. They were all assembled in the council hall to hear his speech.

As the candidate worked up to his finale, the crowd was getting increasingly excited. "I promise better education opportunities for Native Americans!" he declared. And the crowd went wild, shouting "Hoya! Hoya!"

Encouraged by their enthusiasm, the candidate shouted, "I promise gambling reforms to allow a casino on the reservation!"

"Hoya! Hoya!" cried the crowd, stomping their feet.

"I promise more social reforms and job opportunities for Native Americans!"

The crowd reached a frenzied pitch, shouting, "Hoya! Hoya! Hoya!"

After the speech, the politician was touring the reservation and saw a herd of cattle. Feigning interest in the livestock, he asked the chief if he could get a closer look at the herd.

"Sure," the chief said, "but be careful not to step in the *hoya*."

"It's a good speech—just a couple of points need obfuscation."

As philosopher Harry Frankfurt, the pioneer in bull-scatology, notes, bullshit is ultimately far more insidious than outright lying, precisely because it is harder to detect.

Like Frankfurt, we have been guided on our mission by the principal disciplines of philosophy: logic, epistemology, Aristotelian rhetoric here and there, plus a dash of that erstwhile philosophical province now known as psychology. It turns out those courses we took as schoolboys, which appeared at the time to have no use outside of dimly lit coffee shops, are just the trick for decrypting political doublespeak.

LINGUISTIC ANALYSIS

One of our favorite modern philosophers is the Oxford linguistic analyst and Comedy Central star Jon Stewart, who explained, "Yesterday, the president met with a group he calls the 'Coalition of the Willing.' Or, as the rest of the world calls them, Britain and Spain."

The field of logic—much of it rooted in the writings of the early Greeks—demonstrates what rules need to be followed to go from true propositions to correct conclusions. Or to put it the other way around, it shows how we can be tricked by logical fallacies, what logicians call formal fallacies. Epistemology instructs us in what we can deem knowable and why, including how we can sensibly talk about what we are able to know. That field has given rise to conceptual analysis, a rigorous technique for analyzing language and, well, digging out bullshit in all its varieties. As to rhetoric and psychology, they show how our minds and emotions can be manipulated by loaded language.

The *Compact Oxford English Dictionary* defines *fallacy* as "a failure in reasoning that makes an argument invalid."

Fallacies come in two models, *formal* and *informal*. A number of the fallacies in this book are *formal fallacies*: arguments that break one of the technical rules of how a valid argument must be *formed*. For example, there's the fallacy called denying the antecedent. Here's an illustration of how this one goes:

If someone is in Congress, then he or she is
   a U.S. citizen.
President Bush is not in Congress.
Therefore, President Bush is not a U.S. citizen.

We won't be using President Bush's demonstrated noncitizenship to call for his impeachment, however, because the argument is obviously not valid—despite the fact that the premises are both true. That's because the *form* of it is invalid. It's in the form called denying the antecedent, which is expressed in logical notation like this:

If p [the antecedent], then q [the consequent].
Not p.
Therefore, not q.

We can substitute anything at all for p and q, and the argument will always be invalid.

Most of the fallacies in this book are *informal fallacies*, failures in reasoning caused by something other than violations of logical form, say using a lousy analogy or appealing to emotions. Our favorite is the *argumentum ad baculum*, or "argument from the stick," which goes something like this:

MOE: The fairest tax code would be one that only taxes bald people.

LARRY: [smacks Moe in the chops] Nyuk, nyuk!

Many of these fallacies, formal and informal, were identified by Aristotle nearly twenty-five hundred years ago. Has that stopped politicians from using them? On the contrary, they've treated them as formal and informal *strategies*!

But hold the phone! Lest anyone think this stuff is dry as a prairie patty, you should know that we are of the Philogag School of Philosophy, the school that maintains that any philosophical concept worth understanding has a great gag lurking inside it. As we shovel our way through the political patty field, we will uncover not only deceptions, but—more importantly—jokes that point at them and say "Gotcha!"

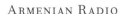

Armenian Radio

During the Soviet era, many of us took smug pleasure in pointing an Orwellian finger at the preposterous disinformation emanating from the Kremlin. But alas, as the world turns, so has that finger.

So it is that some of the gags once whispered in the Soviet Bloc have a certain resonance for us today. The mythical Armenian Radio was an underground treasure trove of absurdist riddles about government-sponsored doublespeak. Among our favorites:

QUESTION FROM ARMENIAN CITIZEN: Is it true that last Sunday Akopian won a hundred thousand rubles in the state lottery?

ANSWER FROM GOVERNMENT SPOKESMAN: Yes, it is true. Only it was not last Sunday, but Monday. And it was not Akopian, but Bagramyan. And not in the state lottery, but in checkers. And not a hundred thousand, but one hundred rubles. And not won, but lost.

Q: Are there any questions you can't answer?
A: No. We approach our job in accordance with Marxist dialectics. To any question we give any answer.

There are loads of things we don't know about the political bullshitters, including just how conscious they are of the errors in reasoning they regularly loft in our direction. But

"*Congratulations, Dave! I don't think I've ever read a more beautifully evasive and subtly misleading public statement in all my years in government.*"

given that so many of them appear to have no qualms about throwing outright lies at us, we tend to believe that even the ones who are verbally challenged know what they are doing.

Finally, a word about the folks we've chosen to quote and the quotes we've chosen from them. We've cast our net to include not only politicos but also their defenders and camp followers—pundits, talking heads, political scientists, reporters, and attorneys. Fact is, they all speak from the same script. As to the quotes themselves, when we've had to choose between deceptive words that led to dangerous and dire consequences (say those that led us into war) and deceptive words with less dangerous consequences, *yet which better demonstrate how the deception was pulled off*, we chose the latter. We figure it's more important to get the clearest possible insight into how politicos perpetrate their tricks than to review the damage they've done. Unfortunately, most of us already know all too well about that damage.

A Chinese proverb proclaims, "Give a man a fish and he will eat for a day. Give a man a fishing pole and he will eat for a lifetime."

For BS digging, we offer a spade—which we call a spade.

PART I

—٣ळ—

The Tricky Talk Strategy
Misleading with Doublespeak

TEXAS SHARPSHOOTER FALLACY

A truly clever politico, one worthy of being called a Great Deceiver, knows that a good way of stupefying us is with verbal sleight of hand. It distracts us from a multitude of deficiencies—like deficient truth. And one artful way of slipping deficient truth into an argument is by *reframing the entire context of what makes a statement true*, the old Epistemological Presto Change-O.

Consider three baseball umpires discussing their calling:

UMPIRE 1: I call 'em the way I sees 'em!
UMPIRE 2: I call 'em the way they are!
UMPIRE 3: They ain't nothin' until I calls 'em!

Umpire 3 is a man who understands that it is within his authority to define reality any way he sees fit.

So is Dick Cheney. Like any good double-talker, he knows how to exploit the Texas sharpshooter ploy, or, as it is known to logicians, the Texas sharpshooter *fallacy*. The vice president or, as he is known to logicians, the vice pseudologist, is particularly adept at this ploy:

> *Well, I look at it and see it is actually an affirmation that there are parts of Iraq where things are going pretty well. In fact, I talked to a friend just the other day who had driven from Baghdad down to Basra, seven hours, found the situation dramatically improved from a year or so ago, sort of validated the British view they had made progress in southern Iraq and that they can therefore reduce their force levels.*
> — Vice President DICK CHENEY, commenting on the news that the British would begin withdrawing their troops from Iraq, February 2007

> *We view this as a success.*
> — Spokesman for U.S. National Security Council GORDON JOHNDROE, commenting on the same news, February 2007

How do you spin an excruciatingly devastating setback? Say you're in a war that you've sold as a conflict between a "Coalition of the Willing" and a "terrorist threat." Say that "terrorist threat" is looking more and more like a civil war. Say there is only one other member of your coalition that was

* *

willing to commit a significant number of troops in the first place. Say that other country has just announced it's about to begin withdrawing its troops from the conflict. Say this happens just at the time when you are struggling to convince your nation that it should be sending *more* troops into battle. What a predicament, huh?

Not if you're an old Texas sharpshooter. You just pull out that trick you used as a kid to impress your friends with your marksmanship. You shoot a bunch of holes in the barn door and *then* draw a target around them. *"See that, guys? Got a bull's-eye every time!"* You say the outcome you've been handed was what you were aiming for all along. Presto change-o, failure becomes success.

It's as if (to pick a random example of the Texas sharpshooter fallacy) after shooting his host, Harry Whittington, in the face, neck, and chest with birdshot on the Armstrong Ranch in south Texas, Cheney had said, "This validates our foreign policy of shoot first, ask questions later."

In the case of the sanguine Gordon Johndroe, he went on to say that "conditions in Basra have improved sufficiently that they are able to transition more control to the Iraqis. . . . The United States shares the same goal of turning responsibility over to the Iraqi Security Forces and reducing the number of American troops in Iraq."

Okay, let's give the devil his due. According to most commentators, the situation in Basra really had improved to the point that a pullout of troops made sense. But shouldn't a willing member of a coalition offer to redeploy those troops to an area where things are not going so well? Say, Baghdad or Anbar, where the Decider-in-Chief was about to commit 21,500 additional U.S. troops?

No??

Bull's-eye!

IGNORATIO ELENCHI
(Ignorance of the Issue)

One of the grand masters of political double-talk is former secretary of defense Donald Rumsfeld, a man who not only vilified the press for missing the point (i.e., *his* point) but who depended on them (and everyone else) to miss the point so he could win an argument. Consider this reference to a classic of the genre:

> *By the afternoon on Wednesday [after September 11], Secretary Rumsfeld was talking about broadening the objectives of our response [to Al-Qaeda] and "getting Iraq." Secretary Powell pushed back, urging a focus on Al-Qaeda . . . [but]* **Rumsfeld complained that there were no decent targets for bombing in Afghanistan and that we should consider bombing Iraq, which, he said, had better targets.**[*]
>
> — RICHARD CLARKE, *Against All Enemies: Inside America's War on Terror*

---

[*] Emphasis ours in all uses of bold italics in quoted materials.

Better targets? Clarke couldn't believe his ears:

*"I thought I was missing something here," I vented [to
Colin Powell]. "Having been attacked by al Qaeda, for
us now to go bombing Iraq in response would be like our
invading Mexico after the Japanese attacked us at Pearl
Harbor."*

Rumsfeld is here employing the old con known as *ignoratio
elenchi* ("ignorance of the issue," perhaps better translated
in this case as "ignoring the issue"). At cocktail parties and
in the bedroom, it is called "missing the point" or "changing
the subject." In *ignoratio elenchi*, the trick is to make a point
that may in itself be valid ("the military always prefers to
strike the most accessible targets") but to use it to support
a completely unrelated conclusion ("so let's strike a totally
different country that has more accessible targets"). It's the
same tactic used in a murder trial by a prosecutor who goes
on at length about how gory the murder was, a point that
has nothing whatsoever to do with the guilt or innocence of
the accused.

Clarke told CBS's *60 Minutes* that at first he thought Mr.
Rumsfeld was joking, an apt response considering there actually is a classic joke that nails this *ignoratio:*

A guy is taking his evening walk when he sees his friend, Joe,
down on his hands and knees under a streetlamp. "What are
you looking for, Joe?" he asks.

"I dropped my car keys," Joe replies.

"Right here?"

"No, over there in the bushes. But the light's better here."

A common example of the-light's-better-here phenom-enon is found in the daily stock market report in the media. It purports to apprise us of how the economy is doing that day, but any economist will tell you that it reveals only a fraction of the total economic picture; we hear no daily reports, for example, on the number of Americans who fell below the poverty line or lost their jobs that day. The reason for that is not simply political spin; it's because those numbers are not available on a daily basis, as they are much harder to measure. It's much easier to read the numbers on the Big Board in the New York Stock Exchange. The light's better in there.

ARGUMENTUM AD ODIUM
(Argument from Hatred)

Neither Mr. Rumsfeld nor most of his colleagues are mut-tonheads, so how does it happen that he could present to them such a crazy argument? Could it be that Rumsfeld was count-ing on the fact that, to this administration, *Iraq* was a dirty word, and dirty words cover a multitude of lapses in logic? This double-talk strategy is known as the "argument from hatred," or *argumentum ad odium*. Simply put, it is a fallacy in which someone tries to win an argument by exploiting existing feelings of bitterness and spite. These feelings, of course, were in large supply following the tragic events of 9/11. Anger and spite were in the air.

Rumsfeld presumably would not have argued for invading Mexico in 1941, despite Clarke's correct assessment that the two situations are logically similar. That's because Mexico lacked one factor: *odium*. Nobody in the United States was angry at Mexicans. But Iraq was a different story: We had already been at war with the Iraqis only a few years earlier, so we had *odium ad nauseam*. The fact that Rumsfeld could recommend (and many of his colleagues could accept) his otherwise wacky argument demonstrates the level of that odium.

ARGUMENTUM AD IGNORANTIAM
(Argument from Ignorance)

Just when we thought Rummy couldn't top himself (with, say, a choice bit of double-talk) he did—with triple-talk:

> *The absence of evidence is not the evidence of absence. . . .*
> *Simply because you do not have evidence that something*
> *does exist does not mean that you have evidence that it*
> *doesn't exist.*

— Former secretary of defense DONALD RUMSFELD,
on WMD in Iraq

With this, Secretary Rumsfeld executes the rhetorical equivalent of the triple lutz. In the guise of instructing us about the folly of one fallacy, he slips in a far subtler fallacy. Sheer genius, R.

But let's start with the fallacy that Mr. Rumsfeld nails on the head. It's called the "argument from ignorance" (*argumentum ad ignorantiam*) and it goes like this: Not knowing that a statement is true is taken to be proof that it is false. He is saying that those who argue that Iraq has no weapons of mass destruction from the fact that none have been found are making a nasty, logical mistake. It is a mistake along the same lines as those evil medievals who once said, "I see no evidence that the earth revolves around the sun, so it must not." It just ain't necessarily so, and the secretary has made a solid point here.

Senator Joseph McCarthy was a master of the use of *argumentum ad ignorantiam*. In claiming one government official was a Communist, he said, "I do not have much information on this except the general statement of the agency that there is nothing in the files to disprove his Communist connections." *Gotcha!*

But Rumsfeld is correct only up to a point. There comes a time when the absence of evidence really *does* become evidence of absence. Copernicus had plenty of evidence that the earth revolves around the sun; it just wasn't common-sense evidence. Had he not been able to produce *any* evidence at all of *any* sort, then we *would* be justified in arguing that his theory should be assumed to be false.

★ ★

WHEN ABSENCE IS EVIDENCE

Two archaeologists, a Greek and an Egyptian, are arguing over who came from the more advanced ancient civilization. The Greek says, "While digging in Corinth, we found copper wires buried under the village. This proves we already had telephones in the sixth century BCE!"

And the Egyptian replies, "Well, in Giza, we dug under the ancient village and found no wires at all, thus proving they had already gone wireless!"

That's why most of us do not believe in the existence of gremlins or mermaids or fairies—we have no reasonable evidence of any kind that they exist. Mr. Rumsfeld might want to reply, "Wait a minute, the absence of evidence is not evidence of absence," about gremlins too. Our advice: *"You don't want to go there, Mr. Secretary."*

Sam Harris, a contemporary philosopher and one of the so-called New Atheists, makes the same point against agnosticism:

> *[Agnostics say] you can't prove a negative (so far so good). Science has no way to disprove the existence of a supreme being (this is strictly true). . . . [But] as my colleague, the physical chemist Peter Atkins, puts it, we must be equally agnostic about the theory that there is a teapot in orbit*

"Oh damn, it was a mirage!"

*around the planet Pluto. We can't disprove it. But that
doesn't mean the theory that there is a teapot is on level
terms with the theory that there isn't.*

So the only reasonable question is, What is the evidence *for*
the existence of WMD? Given sufficient time and lacking *any*
evidence, we can argue for their absence without committing
the fallacy of *argumentum ad ignorantiam*—on the basis that, if
they were there, they probably would have turned up by now.

THE SOFT SIDE OF RUMMY:
HIS FAVORITE NURSERY RHYME

> Yesterday upon the stair
> I met a man who wasn't there.
> He wasn't there again today.
> Oh how I wish he'd go away.

— HUGHES MEARNS

FALLACY OF FALSE DILEMMA

You may be wondering how we could get this far without
quoting George Walker Bush. There is a philosophical reason
for that. A statement can be logically deconstructed if it commits errors in reasoning that lead to false conclusions, but a
statement that makes no sense whatsoever, that appears to be
simply as random an arrangement of words as those typed by

a monkey on a PC keyboard, does not lend itself to any kind of cogent analysis. All the philosopher can say is "Whaaaa?"

Fortunately, here and there, G.W. has uttered some statements that actually do make some kind of sense, albeit *bad* sense, yet sense enough to be worthy of deconstruction. The president's use of the fallacy of the false dilemma is one happy instance:

> *Every nation, in every region, now has a decision to make.*
> *Either you are with us, or you are with the terrorists.*
> — President GEORGE W. BUSH, in a televised address to a joint
>   session of Congress, September 20, 2001

Looked at from a purely logical point of view, this statement clearly commits the fallacy of the false dilemma. Being with us or being with the terrorists are *not* the only options. Another possibility is being for neither. (In some cases this is called neutrality.)

Setting up a false dilemma is a nifty way for a politician to stack the deck. Consider these examples:

> *Will you reelect the ruling party, or will you invite*
> *another attack on New York? Take your pick—*
> *it's one or the other.*

and

> *Are you with us or with the forces of the petroleum*
> *monopoly?*

A scrupulous speaker will not omit any possibilities when setting up conceivable outcomes. Consider the master locutor Donald Rumsfeld, who famously stated, "We do know of certain knowledge that he [Osama bin Laden] is either in Afghanistan, or in some other country, or dead." That seems to cover all the possibilities, to the point of absurdity; he's not really giving us any new information at all. Or maybe Rumsfeld actually was stacking the deck. One possibility he failed to mention was that Osama never existed in the first place.

But a look at another common use of the false dilemma sheds light on how this apparent fallacy can be used nonfallaciously.

Are you going to mow the lawn or are you going to sit there all day?

— Mom, to son

Mom in this scenario obviously knows there are lots of other possibilities besides the two she offers. But the son, if he's wise, will not reply, "Jeez, Mom, what about the possibility of sitting here for the morning and then lying down for most of the afternoon and then going to a movie?" He doesn't answer that way because he knows his mom is creating a dilemma all right, but it's all too real. She's really saying, in effect, "All other options besides mowing the lawn right this minute are off the table, and any other option, as far as I'm concerned, is virtually the same as choosing to sit there all day. Why isn't this a false dilemma, Sonny Boy? *Because I say it isn't!*"

Bush was playing the Mom card. What he meant was, "I am decreeing that either you choose to be with us, or we—the U.S.A.—are going to treat you as if you chose to be with the terrorists."

But of course, "You're either with us or with them!" is a far punchier way of putting it. And for better or for worse (and everything in between), much of the international community thought better than to nitpick the logic of his formulation.

Another little-known—and totally unrelated—fallacy of false alternatives is illustrated in this old world joke:

> Two beggars are sitting a few feet apart on a busy street in a notoriously anti-Semitic neighborhood. One has a sign that reads PLEASE HELP A WOUNDED WAR VETERAN. The other's sign reads HELP A POOR OLD JEW.
>
> Hundreds of people pass by during the day. Just to spite the Jew, even those who would never ordinarily give money to a beggar make a big show of putting large sums of money into the war veteran's cup.
>
> Finally, a good man passes by, gives money equally to both, and says to the Jew, "Look, why don't you change your sign? I hate to say it, but people around here don't particularly like Jews. With a sign like that, you're never going to get a penny."

When the good man is out of earshot, the old Jew turns to the other beggar and says, "Get a load of him, Moishe. Look who's trying to teach *us* about business!"

WEASEL WORDS

Often the trickiest con job is the most in-your-face con job. Take weasel words, in which a term is replaced with a less loaded or squishier term right in front of your eyes. When they're used deftly, you don't know what hit you. Consider this bit of weaseling perpetrated by a government official dedicated to preventing sneak attacks:

> CNN INTERVIEWER: *You know, going back to September 2001, the president said, dead or alive, we're going to get [Osama bin Laden]. Still don't have him. I know you are saying there's successes on the war on terror, and there have been. That's a failure.*

> HOMELAND SECURITY ADVISOR FRANCES FRAGOS TOWNSEND: *Well, I'm not sure—it's a success that hasn't occurred yet. I don't know that I view that as a failure.*

Thanks for the heads-up, Ms. Townsend. You've opened up an entire world of options for perilous situations. Like: "I'm not drunk, officer. What you're seeing is sobriety that hasn't returned yet." And: "I'm not driving without a license either! If you must know, I'm driving *with* a license that I don't yet have." Or: "No, dear, I didn't lose my job. I prefer to think of it as a promotion that hasn't occurred yet."

Weasel words are so called because of the weasel's ability to suck the contents out of an egg without breaking the shell. Weasel words are a particular form of equivocation, designed to neutralize a statement or avoid a commitment. So we don't *withdraw* troops, we *redeploy* them. We don't *escalate* a war, we have a *surge*. And in the example at hand, we didn't *fail*, we *anticipate success*. The Homeland Security advisor here elevates weaseling to its ne plus ultra, substituting a word's near opposite for its original meaning. This is a trick worthy of the best egg-suckers, and one that George Orwell saw coming when he coined the term *Newspeak*.

By labeling Ms. Townsend's statement an equivocation, we have granted it some measure of truth, marginal as that may be; that is to say, it is ridiculously misleading, but not an out-and-out falsehood. But at what point does equivocation cross the line from an insistent commitment to a position that is patently false?

So this guy is walking down Main Street when he sees another fellow. He stops him and says, "Rappaport! What happened to you? You used to be a short, fat man, and now you're a tall, skinny man. You used to be so well dressed and clean, and now you're dressed in filthy old clothes. You used to be bald, and now you've got a full head of hair."

"I am not Rappaport," says the other fellow.

And the first guy retorts, "So, you changed your name too!"

Frank Luntz, a Republican consultant, has written an entire book about weaseling, called *Words That Work*. He counsels politicians to say:

electronic intercepts	NOT	*wiretapping*
exploring for energy	NOT	*drilling for oil*
tax simplification	NOT	*tax reform*
tax relief	NOT	*tax cuts*
opportunity scholarships	NOT	*vouchers*

The Democrats are not above the fray. Liberal linguist George Lakoff, tired of being outflanked by the clever conservatives who substitute *death tax* for *estate tax*, tries his hand at counterweaseling—how about *freedom judges* instead of *judicial activists*? he asks. Nice try, George, but the conservatives are obviously better at this.

It's easy to see why politicians would pay big bucks for this kind of advice. Here's some for free:

NEVER SAY:	SAY INSTEAD:
"My mother was an ax-murderer."	"My mother was a cutlery specialist."
"I spent seven years in Leavenworth and three months at the Betty Ford Center."	"I received my education in some of the most venerable institutions in our nation."
"I started out as a bartender in a gentlemen's club."	"I have always striven to serve the public."

"Let's change 'brink of chaos' to 'Everything is wonderful.'"

But hold the phone! Is Ms. Townsend only guilty of weasel-wording, or has she also committed a variation on the aforementioned argument from ignorance? In this variant, something is supposedly true simply because it hasn't been proven false *yet*. No one has proven that Osama will *never* be caught, so, according to Townsend's argument, that means we can assume he will be—and that's a success if she ever saw one.

"How's that again, Ms. T.?"

But don't get us wrong, we're not poking fun at this logic. We're actually lauding it. Just not *yet*.

A recently identified species of weasel words was given the moniker *Unspeak* by writer Steven Poole, in his book of the same name. Unspeak involves the tactic of renaming political positions to contain hidden values. Here are some tricky examples of Unspeak in action:

> *I hope every woman in this country, whether they agree with* Roe *or they disagree with* Roe, *whether they themselves would make one decision or another, will come together and say: Pro-choice means that the Government respects the individual, and isn't that really what our country is all about?*
> — BARBARA BOXER, U.S. senator

> *We are collecting affidavits from women who have been harmed by abortion, from women who are convinced that authentic feminism is pro-life, and from professionals who*

* *

know that Roe *has weakened the moral fabric of the legal and medical professions.*

— NORMA MCCORVEY, the "Jane Roe" who was the winning plaintiff in the court case *Roe v. Wade* (establishing the right to abortion) but who is currently a pro-life feminist

Does anybody remember when *pro-life* was called *anti-abortion?* And when *pro-choice* was dubbed *for abortion* or, more explicitly, *for abortion on demand?*

Those were the good old days before the term reframers got hold of the English language and renamed political positions and arguments to contain loaded and hidden arguments. In the 1970s, the anti-abortionists took on the label *right-to-lifers*, which they recently refined to *pro-lifers*. The genius of this rechristening is that it casts their opponents as *anti-lifers* or, even better, *pro-deathers*. Thus, the choice between being a pro-lifer and a pro-deather became like the choice, "Who would you rather be, Luke Skywalker or Darth Vader?"

The pro-abortion-on-demanders needed a name change— quick—and came up with *pro-choice*. Their new moniker also contained an unspoken universally American value: *choice.* It is positively un-American to be against choice, this being a free country and all. (Unfortunately for the pro-choicers, the term is also loaded with a hint of consumerism, as if choosing whether or not to bring a pregnancy to term were akin to choosing whether or not to buy a high-definition TV.)

A great advantage of hidden arguments is that they rarely get argued. For starters, are all pro-lifers pacifists? Or for that matter, are they all against the death penalty? No way. So just how inclusive is their pro-life position? It is fundamentally limited to fetuses, but admitting that would bring them back to being just old-fashioned anti-abortionists.

Likewise, are all pro-choicers—liberal as they might be—for untrammeled freedom of choice, say the freedom to fill in wetlands or to pack an assault weapon? Not.

Nonetheless, these neologisms stick. They become the accepted terms of discourse for television commentators, political debaters, and Starbucks klatches. And the end result is people routinely arguing with terms that already posit and grant fundamental positions.

The following terms are included in Steven Poole's extensive list of unspeakably sneaky Unspeak:

- *intelligent design* for *creationism* (as if an "Intelligent Designer" might be someone less religious than "the Creator");
- *surge* for *escalation* (not only does *surge* sound less ominous, it has a faintly sexual loading);
- *sound science* for, well, *science* (the folks at Philip Morris are responsible for coining this one, which contains the hidden supposition that there are all kinds of sciences to choose from, including, say, unsound science—you know, the one that insists there is a connection between smoking and cancer).

And here's one of our own favorites: *preventing voter fraud* for *disenfranchising poor and minority potential voters*.

ARTFUL EQUIVOCATION

As a rule, politicians prep for their careers by going to law school (there are exceptions, of course, like Tom DeLay, who went to exterminator school). At law school, these budding double-talkers learn the invaluable art of parsing language with dizzying precision. The weird thing is that, often, the more precise the language gets, the more equivocal and laughable it is.

Needless to mention, former president William Jefferson Clinton was an outstanding student at Yale Law School, although not quite as brilliant as his classmate Hillary Rodham.

> *It depends on what the meaning of the word* is *is.*
>
> — President BILL CLINTON, explaining to a grand jury why he was not lying when he told his top aides, in regard to Monica Lewinsky, "There is nothing between us."

First of all, as hilarious as Mr. Clinton's statement sounds, it is grammatically on target. Whether or not he was lying to his staff *does* depend on whether we take his use of the word *is* ("there *is* nothing between us") to be in the simple present tense or in the present continuous tense. We use the simple present tense for events that happen regularly, as in "I get up each morning at 6:00," or for permanent situations, as in "I am an American." We use the continuous present tense to talk about events that are actually happening "around about now." Mr. Clinton is asserting (with a straight face) that he was using the continuous present tense when he said, "There is nothing between us"—meaning that *at that particular moment and the surrounding moments*, he and Ms. Lewinsky were a non-item.

FUN WITH AMBIGUITY

"There was a beautiful young woman knocking on my hotel room door all night! I finally had to let her out."
— DAN'S UNCLE DIGBY

The reason Clinton's legalistic argument sounds so funny is because it reminds us of the gambits kids employ to mess up their parents' minds without outright lying. "Did you give some serious thought to your science project this afternoon?" "Sure did, Mom!" Translation: "While I was dancing in my room to Beyoncé's new video, I glanced over at my science project and realized it looked kind of puny." Or more on topic, consider the college sophomore who insists to her parents that she is not sleeping with her boyfriend (euphemisms like *sleeping with* are a gold mine for quibblers).

What Bill and the young people are doing is not precisely lying, as they would adamantly argue, but equivocating. They are exchanging one meaning of the word *is* (or the words *sure did* or *sleeping with*) for another meaning that they hope we will bring to bear on our interpretation of their answer.

George Burns and Gracie Allen built their entire television act around just this sort of slipperiness of the meanings of words:

GEORGE: *Where did you get the flowers?*
GRACIE: *I went to visit Mabel in the hospital.*
GEORGE: *So?*
GRACIE: *Well, you told me to take her flowers.*
GEORGE: *Say goodnight, Gracie.*
GRACIE: *Goodnight, Gracie.*

Say goodnight, Bill.

ARGUMENT FROM WEAK ANALOGY

When other double-talk strategies fail, a gifted political con artist brings out the old argument from analogy, which is basically saying, "Hmm, X—that reminds me of a very instructive story about Y, which is pretty much the same deal, so it proves my point about X."

Often, of course, Y is *not* the same deal as X in critical respects, so the Y story is not very instructive at all. In that case, logicians call this an argument from *weak* analogy.

This bill reminds me of legislation that ought to be introduced to outlaw automobiles [because they kill people too].
— Former representative (and former owner of an extermination business) TOM DELAY, in an attack on a congressional bill to ban the carcinogen chlordane from use in termite control

Look, Al-Qaeda, they could bring in a nuke into this country and kill 100,000 people with a well-placed nuke somewhere. OK. We would recover from that. It would be

*a terrible tragedy, but the teachers' unions in this country
can destroy a generation.*

— Libertarian commentator NEAL BOORTZ, in an attack on
   teachers' unions in an interview on Fox News' *Hannity & Colmes*

*It's kind of like we're in the fourth quarter of a football
game and you're the quarterback and your team is
way ahead here in the fourth quarter and opponents are
very desperate, trying to sack you, and aren't doing
a very good job of it. And they haven't hit you all day
now for two days. And you're going to keep getting
these last-minute Hail Marys thrown at you. So just
bear with us.*

— Senator CHUCK GRASSLEY, on the progress of the Alito
   Supreme Court nomination hearings

Our main point is that a weak analogy is like a congress-
person stumbling in a hailstorm. Don't ask—it wouldn't help
anyhow. And that *is* our point.

A few years ago, we started collecting colorful similes
(a type of analogy) that don't lead anywhere in particular but are, like, funny. Here are a few of our latest
additions:

• *Her artistic sense was exquisitely refined, like someone who
  can tell butter from I Can't Believe It's Not Butter.*

ONE PERSON'S WEAK ANALOGY
IS ANOTHER PERSON'S PERFECT FIT

"I don't care if she is a tape dispenser. I love her."

- *She walked into my office like a centipede with ninety-eight missing legs.*
- *She grew on him like she was a colony of microbes and he was room-temperature beef.*
- *The lamp just sat there like an inanimate object.*

An analogy operates on the inference that if things are similar in some respects, they are similar in others. But before differentiating between strong and weak analogies, it is necessary to understand that by definition, *no* analogy is perfect; if it were perfect, it would not be an analogy, but an identity—that is, the two things compared would be the same in *all* respects rather than in just *some* respects. So in an absolute sense, all analogies are somewhat weak, i.e., imperfect. But heaven knows, some are weaker than others.

The weakest analogies display one or both of the two following failings:

1. The supposed *primary points of similarity* between the things or events being compared are tenuous.

2. The supposed *inferred points of similarity* simply don't follow.

Between any two objects, no matter how different, there are always *some* similarities—far-fetched as they may be. For example, Lewis Carroll once posed to his readers the following nonsense riddle: "How is a raven like a writing desk?"

The point of his riddle was that they are *not* alike in any way. But to Carroll's surprise, one reader came up with a clever solution: "Poe wrote on both."[i]

Let's get back to the Exterminator's analogy between the carcinogenic potential of a particular termite poison and the lethal potential of automobiles in our streets. DeLay is quite right to say the two are similar in the sense that they both have the potential to kill human beings. But obviously missing from his analogy is the statistical likelihood of each form of death. Our guess is that you get far more fatalities per chlordane-sprinkled house than per car on the road. What's more, DeLay omits a cost-benefit analysis. Again, it's only our guess, but we imagine that doing without chlordane—even if it meant doing *with* termites—would have less of a deleterious impact on the quality of our lives today than doing without automobiles would. So clearly there are crucial points of dissimilarity that are missing from the analogy, undoubtedly because they just don't wash. Way weak, Tom.

As for Mr. Boortz, he apparently wants us to believe that, because teachers' unions supposedly do more harm than terrorists with nukes, we should root them out with even greater fervor. His inference works: *If* his preposterous premise were true, we probably *would* be obliged to ban teachers' unions. The weakness is in the alleged point of similarity.

What DeLay's and Boortz's weak analogies have in common is that they are both over-the-top appeals to emotion. DeLay is going after our sense of fear by implying that if you forbid chlordane just because it sometimes kills people, next thing we know you'll be forbidding slam-dancing for the same reason, and then—who knows?—getting out of bed in the morning because it's been demonstrated that you are far more likely to be hit by an errant bullet if you get out of bed than if you stay there. Forbidding cars doesn't appear so unlikely in this context, does it? You have every reason to be afraid of encroaching government control, or what one libertarian has dubbed the "Nanny State."

For Boortz, the emotional appeal is far simpler: Are you afraid of terrorists? You should be way more afraid of teachers' unions.

As to Senator Grassley's analogy between the nomination hearings and his football fantasy, we're only guessing that it's weak—we fell asleep in the third quarter.

SLIPPERY SLOPE ARGUMENT

These days, warnings of "sliding down a slippery slope" are all the rage for politicos, pundits, mothers, and restaurant owners. It's the classic one-thing-leads-to-another-and-before-you-know-it-you're-in-deep-doo-doo argument. The beauty part of this argument is that you can lay down just about any outcome at the bottom of the slope as long as you stipulate quasi-believable steps along the way.

*If the Supreme Court says that you have the right to con-
sensual [gay] sex within your home, then you have the
right to bigamy, you have the right to polygamy, you have
the right to incest, you have the right to adultery. You have
the right to anything.*

— Former senator RICK SANTORUM

The slippery slope argument contends that event A will
trigger a chain reaction of events leading, eventually, to an
undesirable event. But what is important to keep in mind is
that not *all* SSAs are fallacious, not even—from a certain per-
spective—Senator Santorum's.

In a *valid* slippery slope argument, event A *logically entails* the
chain reaction that leads to the wolf-infested ravine at the bottom of the slope. Perhaps Santorum's reasoning goes like this:

1. The Supreme Court seems to be saying that a consen-
   sual sexual relationship in the privacy of one's home is
   protected under the Constitution.

2. If that's so, then the sexual relationship called bigamy
   is logically protected too. So is polygamy. So is incest.
   So is adultery.

Hmmm. Could it be that there is something slippery about
Santorum's logic, say in the scope of his premise? The only
way Santorum's argument could be valid logically is if the
sole consideration in deciding the constitutionality of protecting *any* sexual relationship in the home is the *right to*

privacy. Actually, one could make a pretty good case before the Supreme Court that, in fact, that *is* the case with adultery. That's a private matter between consenting adults, so it's protected, end of story. But it would be a little chancier, if not totally crazy, to argue that's also the case with incest between consenting adults. Considerations other than the related lovers' privacy have to be taken into account, like how their actions affect their other relatives or the chance they could produce a genetically screwed-up child. And there's no ambiguity concerning the presence of extraprivacy issues in bigamy and polygamy. Both of these are arrangements that are not exclusively, or even primarily, sexual, and they clearly have all kinds of implications, including legal ones, that involve other people, like the family's children. So we cannot give Santorum a total pass into the realm of the logically valid slippery slope argument after all.

But there can be a realm other than logic for judging the validity of an SSA argument—the psychological realm—and like most psychological judgments, this one is always dicey, which is to say, psychological SSAs can never be argued *conclusively*. They always slip into the category of *maybe true, but then again, maybe not.*

Consider the joke about the restaurant owner from Toledo:

Two men are sitting facing each other on a train. One is an older businessman who is going over his accounts. Occasionally he looks at a gold Omega watch on his wrist.

* *

The other is much younger and is wearing threadbare jeans. After some time, the young man asks, "Excuse me, could you tell me what time it is?"

The older man does not reply.

"Excuse me again, but could you please tell me what time it is?"

The older man looks out the window. Then he looks at the younger man and says, "No!"

The younger man is quite irritated by this: "Look here, I asked you a perfectly civil question. Why don't you tell me the time?"

The older man replies, "If I tell you what time it is, we will start a conversation. You will find out things about me. You will find out that I am the owner of the fanciest restaurant in Toledo, that I have a beautiful, unmarried daughter. You will come to visit us. You will fall in love with my daughter. You will marry her. . . ."

"Well, would this be so terrible? I am a perfectly respectable young man."

"Perhaps," says the older man. "But I don't want a son-in-law who cannot afford a watch!"

All the slips on the slope the restaurant owner creates are pure psychological conjecture. Like just how gorgeous can his daughter be that every young man instantly falls in love with her? We don't know. To tell the truth, we've never seen her—although she certainly sounds very nice, sir. So the point is, maybe telling the young man what time it is would lead to him marrying said daughter. Hey, it could happen. But maybe not also. So don't tell us you're presenting an irrefutable and conclusive argument, big shot.

And that goes for you too, Rick. If your argument is "Once we accept gay sex in the home, it becomes more palatable to the Supreme Court to consider protecting bigamy, etc.," all we can say is maybe yes, maybe no. We don't know the personal psychology of the members of the Supreme Court, especially that one from Toledo.

THE REVERSE SLIPPERY SLOPE

In *On Murder*, Thomas De Quincey wrote, "If once a man indulges himself in murder, very soon he comes to think little of robbing; and from robbing he comes next to drinking and sabbath-breaking, and from that to incivility and procrastination."

That reminds us of another classic story:

A devout Baptist couple meet their pastor at the church to consult on their upcoming wedding. They have a problem on their minds that they need to ask him about.

"Pastor, my fiancée and I really want to dance together at our celebration," says the man. "Can we do that?"

"Absolutely not!" replies the pastor. "Dancing is the devil's work."

"Fine," says the woman. Then a huge question comes to her mind. "What about sex? Can we have sex?"

"Absolutely," says the pastor. "Genesis 1:28 commands us to be fruitful and multiply."

"Uh, how about the woman on top?" asks the man.

"It's all okay, as long as you're fruitful and multiply," replies the pastor.

"On the kitchen table?"

"That doesn't change anything. Go right ahead."

"How about standing up?"

"ABSOLUTELY NOT!" screams the pastor.

"Really? Why not?"

"*That* could lead to dancing!"

DISTINCTION WITHOUT A DIFFERENCE

While running for president, Senator John Kerry said that he is *for* gay civil unions that include all the rights and benefits of marriage but he is *against* gay civil marriage. When a reporter asked him what exactly the difference is between a gay civil union and a gay civil marriage, Kerry gave the following response:

There is a distinction. There's no distinction in the rights that are afforded. The distinction is in a body of America that culturally, historically and religiously views marriage very differently.

* *

Huh? What just happened there? After in effect admitting that there is no difference at all between civil marriage and civil unions—like, where else would you look for a difference except in the "rights that are afforded"?—Kerry goes on to say there *is* in fact a difference.

What has happened, of course, is that Kerry has attempted to con us. Kerry needed to create a difference where there isn't one in order to avoid the unpopular position of being "pro–gay marriage," while at the same time mollifying his base by being "pro–gay civil unions." So he employed the tactic used by politicians since Cain and Abel were favorite son candidates: double-talk.

Kerry was using one of the oldest double-talk gambits in the book, making a distinction without a difference. And he was doing it in a particularly skillful way: by attributing the distinction to that unassailable authority, the American public, thus committing another common fallacy, the appeal to the authority of the many (or, as it was known to confidence men throughout the Roman Empire, the *argumentum ad populum*).

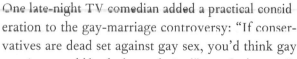

One late-night TV comedian added a practical consideration to the gay-marriage controversy: "If conservatives are dead set against gay sex, you'd think gay marriage would be the best solution!" *But that's a totally different argument.*

"There's nothing wrong with <u>our</u> marriage, but the spectre of gay marriage has hopelessly eroded the institution."

The distinction without a difference fallacy occurs when a particular word or phrase is insisted on in preference to another, even though the new word has the exact same meaning as the old one. The word substitution is usually made because one of the words has emotional connotations the other doesn't. In this case, *union*, even with all the rights and privileges of marriage thrown in, doesn't have the emotional baggage of *marriage*, so—what the heck?—let's make a false distinction between the two labels.

None other than our old friend Senator Rick Santorum came closer than Kerry did to speaking truthiness on this one:

> *[I]f there are laws that the states want to pass having to do with certain benefits or things like that, that's one thing. But "civil union" sounds too much to me like marriage.*

Right, Rick. And the reason they sound alike is that the two terms mean the same thing.

In his attempt to find a basis for his false distinction, Kerry employs the old *argumentum ad populum*: the difference lies in the view of a "body of America." This *arg ad pop*, in effect, posits, "If a distinction between unions and marriages is popular, it must be okay." This is not an argument that should be employed by someone who lost the popular vote.

HIDDEN ASSUMPTION

Any political commentator worthy of having his own

program on Fox News knows that when it comes to hiding the truth, burial is a nifty option. Why risk a blatant, in-your-face fib when a questionable assumption buried in a seemingly logical argument might slip right by the listener? A perennial favorite hidden assumption is that something is morally right because it is "natural," the way Mother Nature intended it.

Consider Bill O'Reilly, on his Fox News program *The O'Reilly Factor*, dismissing scientific research that demonstrates that children suffer no psychological deficit from same-sex parenting:

> *Nature dictates that a dad and a mom is the optimum [form of child rearing]. Why [if there's no psychological deficit] wouldn't Nature then make it that anybody could get pregnant by eating a cupcake?*

Note Mr. O'Reilly's unspoken assumption: The course nature dictates is always optimum *on all counts*. But just because "nature dictates" that it takes a man and a woman to make a baby doesn't necessarily mean that combo is the best when it comes to child rearing. By O'Reilly's reasoning, when it comes to staying warm in winter, running around in our birthday suits would beat wearing clothes. Nature didn't bring us into the world in shiny sports jackets, did it? It didn't even bring us forth in O'Reilly's other favorite garb, sheep's clothing. Furthermore, we have to ask, is using a loofah mitt for foreplay really the method Nature intended?

Naturalistic Fallacy

This particular hidden assumption is rooted in a fallacy so frequently used it has its own name: the naturalistic fallacy, or the appeal to nature—to wit, a claim that something is good or right because it is natural or, inversely, that something is bad or wrong because it is unnatural. The not-always-so-hidden assumption is that nature shows us the ideal or desired way of operating. Like, the best way to travel from New York to Los Angeles is on foot, right? (Interestingly, when the airplane was invented there were those who argued that if God had meant us to fly, he would have given us wings or, at the very least, stewardesses.)

The neat thing about identifying hidden assumptions in general is that once you find them, the arguments based on them often go up in smoke. When we lay out Mr. O'Reilly's whole argument, it looks like this:

1. Whatever nature dictates is best in all respects.
2. Nature dictates that only a man and a woman can have a child.
3. Therefore, a man and a woman must provide the best child rearing.

When the argument is presented in its entirety, it's clear that the hidden assumption—what's natural is in all ways for the best—is way screwy.

We won't comment on Mr. O'Reilly's personal fantasy of impregnation by cupcake. Live and let live, we say.

* *

FRAMING THE DEBATE

Any member of a high school debate team learns the importance of framing the debate, limiting its scope to what is relevant to the subject in question, and hence excluding irrelevant material. But these days the term *framing the debate* has come to mean "stacking the deck so that only stuff that bolsters your own position is allowed to be discussed." You know we're in trouble when the very language used to describe the protocol of evenhanded debate gets weaseled around to describe a slippery debate tactic:

> *The debate should not be about the surge or its details.*
> *This debate should not even be about the Iraq war to date,*
> *mistakes that have been made, or whether we can, or*
> *cannot, win militarily. If we let Democrats force us into a*
> *debate on the surge or the current situation in Iraq, we lose.*

— Excerpt from a memo from Representatives JOHN SHADEGG
(R-AZ) and PETER HOEKSTRA (R-MI) concerning how
to debate a House resolution entitled "Disapproving of the
decision of the President announced on January 10, 2007,
to deploy more than 20,000 additional United States
combat troops to Iraq" (as quoted in the online newsletter
Think Progress)

Here we have framing the debate that jigs the frame down to nanodimensions!

The entire resolution, H. Con. Res. 63, must have set a record for congressional brevity:

1. Congress and the American people will continue to support and protect the members of the United States Armed Forces who are serving or who have served bravely and honorably in Iraq; and

2. Congress disapproves of the decision of President George W. Bush announced on January 10, 2007, to deploy more than 20,000 additional United States combat troops to Iraq.

It already *had* a built-in reframing. First the Republicans had tried to frame the issue to demonstrate that the Democrats were not supporting the troops. But then the Democrats took that frame away from the Republicans and used it to frame *them*: They added the first clause.

The only debatable issue left for the Republicans was the second clause: disapproving of the surge. Representatives Shadegg and Hoekstra's stratagem is breathtaking in its daring: reframe the debate so that it is not about *anything*!

The take-home lesson here is this: When reframing, think boldly!

Thinking Way Inside the Frame: Some Everyday Tips for Reframing

- For discussions with a spouse: *"Of course we should talk about our relationship, darling. But my infidelities, our sex life, trust, money, property, and mutual support are off the table."*

- For conversations with employees: *"The purpose of this meeting, Bob, is to discuss your job performance. Please don't interject things like your contributions to the firm. Frankly, the company has no desire to be put in the position of having to give you a well-deserved raise."*

- For approaching the bench: *"Your Honor, in this trial the sole question before the court should be the length of the defendant's sentence. The counsel for the defense keeps trying to insert his claim that the defendant is innocent. Please consider that if we go down that road, the State will lose."*

THE RHETORIC OF REPARTEE

To end this section on a positive note, there is one form of clever language that employs the devil's tools on the side of the angels—it's called wit:

I do declare, if this be true, General Pinckney has kept them all for himself and cheated me out of my two.

— President JOHN ADAMS, responding in 1798 to a rumor that he had sent Pinckney to England to bring back four mistresses, two for Pinckney and two for himself

HECKLER IN THE CROWD: [yelling at 1928 presidential candidate Al Smith] *Go ahead, Al, don't let me bother you. Tell 'em all you know. It won't take long.*

AL SMITH: *If I tell 'em all we both know, it won't take me any longer.*

> *"JACK, DON'T BUY A SINGLE VOTE MORE*
> *THAN NECESSARY. I'LL BE DAMNED IF I'M*
> *GOING TO PAY FOR A LANDSLIDE."*
> — Presidential candidate JOHN F. KENNEDY, pretending to read
>   a telegram from his father, in response to rumors that Joseph
>   Kennedy was planning to "buy the election" [ii]

But, alas, the times have changed:

> *Go f—k yourself.*
> — Vice President DICK CHENEY to Senator Patrick Leahy, in
>   response to Leahy's criticism of Cheney for Halliburton's
>   alleged war profiteering

What can we say except that it makes us long for the days
before we came to our rhetorical wit's end.

—ᴍ—

The "So's Your Mother" Strategy

Misleading by Getting Personal

In this strategy, the politico throws a new ingredient into the stockpot of tricky language: personal opprobrium, sometimes known as trash, as in *trash talk*. The idea is to supplement misleading language with misleading attributions of ignominy concerning your opponent.

GUILT BY ASSOCIATION

One cunning method of personally attacking your opponent is the bad company technique, or guilt by association. Take, for example, the case of the late reverend Jerry Falwell and his opponent, the *Teletubbies* character Tinky Winky:

> *He is purple—the gay pride color; and his antenna is shaped like a triangle—the gay pride symbol.*
> — FALWELL on Tinky Winky

Reverend Jerry would have had us believe that Tinky Winky is an insidious poster boy for the lifestyle known as "gay," and that Tinky Winky should therefore not only be reviled; he should be knocked off the air.

Oh, where to begin? First of all, let's leave aside the obvious question, "What is so wrong with Tinky Winky being gay or having gay sympathies (except to say that one out of every nine cartoon characters is born gay)?" The clergyman's argument rested on the idea that Tinky and a social group Falwell disapproved of have certain stylistic qualities in common. If Tinky had chosen a swastika as a fashion accessory, we might grant Falwell his point. But the triangular shape of Tinky's antenna? Does this put plane geometry teachers across the country at risk too? In short, Falwell is attributing "guilt" by association, and both the guilt and the association appear to be largely in his mind.

Senator Joseph McCarthy's attack on Edward R. Murrow is a far trickier instance of assigning guilt by association:

And I am compelled by the facts to say to you that Mr. Edward R. Murrow, as far back as twenty years ago, was engaged in propaganda for Communist causes. For example, the Institute of International Education, of which he was the Acting Director, was chosen to act as a representative by a Soviet agency to do a job which would normally be done by the Russian secret police.

— Senator JOSEPH MCCARTHY, HUAC hearings

In this case, the association is with the Institute of International Education, an organization that at one time did business with the Soviet Union. So, according to McCarthy, ipso facto Murrow is a Communist sympathizer and propagandist. In fact, Murrow's work for the IIE was to arrange for European scholars who were at risk in their home countries to lecture and teach at U.S. colleges and universities. At some point this included Soviet scholars. But to McCarthy such details just muddied up his neat equation: If you work with a person from a Communist country, you must be an apparatchik. McCarthy's pièce de résistance is his line stating that Murrow's department at IIE "was chosen to act as a representative by a Soviet agency to do a job which would normally be done by the Russian secret police." That part, of course, is pure fabrication—Murrow's job had nothing whatsoever to do with anybody's policing. But when your job description is to foment guilt by association, you can always fall back on free association.

Sometimes, however, it is we, the audience, rather than the person making the political statement, who commit guilt by association. We should be ashamed of ourselves—we, of all people, should be setting an example for others to mindlessly follow. Consider your reaction to the following:

> *Your water's dying . . . Your trees are dying. Your wildlife's locked up in zoos. You're in the zoo, Man. How do you feel about it?*
> — CHARLES MANSON, murderer and animal-rights activist

It's not often that we get to line up Jerry Falwell, Joseph McCarthy, and Charles Manson on the same list, but we have to admit, it does feel kind of good. The Jerry and Joe quotes commit the bad company fallacy, impugning guilt or disrepute to a party by tying that party to a person or group with a bad rep. Charlie's quote tempts any upstanding citizen to commit a similar error himself, the genetic fallacy.

That Charles Manson is an environmentalist and animal-rights activist certainly seems counterintuitive, but it is not illogical per se. Believing that it's okay to kill people but not to jail animals is not a contradiction, it's just crazy. But the fact that this crazy murderer is for animal rights might lead us to rethink our position vis-à-vis the civil liberties of the four-footed, just as the fact that Hitler was a vegetarian could tempt us to reject the rights of sirloin-supplying mammals. In either case, we would be committing the genetic fallacy, judging the truth or falsehood, or the rightness or wrongness, of a particular proposition on the basis of a person who holds it. But both logical and moral propositions stand or fall on their own, regardless of who else subscribes to them. And you know that if we say that, it's got to be true.

"AD HOMONYM" ARGUMENT

"So's your mother" arguments are often called *ad hominem*, meaning they are directed at the person ("at the man") rather than at the substance of the issue. President Nixon created his own hilarious variation: the *ad homonym* argument, where

* *

guilt—or innocence—by association is based on similar-sounding words. (NB: *ad homonym* is a homonym for *ad hominem*—still with us?)

Admittedly, *ad homonym* arguments occur rarely, but when they do, they can boggle the mind, as seen below. (Note that in common American pronunciation, "Du Bois" [as in W. E. B. Du Bois] rhymes with "rejoice.")

Also note that we don't make this stuff up, and to prove it, we quote directly from a *New York Times* article, dated March 9, 1966:

> Richard M. Nixon decried yesterday the similarity in the pronunciation of the Du Bois Club and the Boys Club of America, saying it misled people into confusing one organization with the other. The former Vice President, who is national board chairman of the Boys Club of America, said in a statement that the confusion was "an almost classic example of Communist deception and duplicity." The Du Bois Club . . . was described as a Communist-front group last Friday by Attorney General Nicholas B. Katzenbach. . . .

TU QUOQUE (YOU TOO!)

A particularly blatant example of the "So's your mother" strategy is *tu quoque*, literally "you too" or "you're another." (We don't know about you, but we find it oddly comforting that there is a Latin term for the rhetorical equivalent of schoolyard name-calling.)

Consider the following colloquy:

Everybody in politics lies, but they [the Clintons] do it with such ease, it's troubling.

— DAVID GEFFEN, Hollywood supermogul, Obama supporter (at the time), and former big-time contributor to the Clintons

If Senator Obama is indeed sincere about his repeated claims to change the tone of our politics, he should immediately denounce these remarks, remove Mr. Geffen from his campaign and return his money.

— HOWARD WOLFSON, Hillary Clinton's communications director, the day Geffen's remark appeared in *The New York Times*

It's not clear to me why I'd be apologizing for someone else's remark.

— BARACK OBAMA, senator, hours after the above comments

It's ironic that the Clintons had no problem with David Geffen when he was raising them $18 million and sleeping at their invitation in the Lincoln Bedroom. It is also ironic that Senator Clinton lavished praise on Monday and is fully willing to accept today the support of South Carolina State Senator Robert Ford, who said if Barack Obama *were to win the nomination, he would drag down the rest of the Democratic Party because "he's black."*

— ROBERT GIBBS, Obama spokesman, same news cycle

It is often said that all of life is high school—over and over again. But we beg to differ, at least when it comes to political rhetoric, where a good part of life is grade school. In particular, the grade school playground, where we still remember hearing such high wit as we find in the following:

"Oh yeah? Well, your mother wears army boots!" (This obviously dates us; we were grade-schoolers before army boots became a hip fashion statement.)

and

"You say I'm stupid? When your IQ reaches 50, you should sell!"

and

"My sister? Your sister is depriving a village somewhere of an idiot."

Happily, the likes of Hillary and Obama and their *tu quoque* deputies keep us from feeling nostalgic for those good old days.

As with all rhetorical strategies, timing is the crucial element. For example, you shouldn't use "you too" until *after* you've been attacked. Otherwise, it seems so—what shall we say?—out of context.

A young man got a flat tire on a lonely country road late at night. He looked in his trunk and discovered he had no jack. So he started out down the road, looking for a farmhouse where he hoped he could borrow one. After walking a mile or so, he saw a light in the distance, but as he approached the house, he began to think, "It's very late and very dark. What's this guy going to think when someone knocks on his door?" The closer he got to the house, the more nervous he got. "He's probably going to tell me to go away. In fact, he's going to yell at me. He'll probably cuss me out." But he felt he had no choice, so he screwed up his courage, went to the door, and knocked. The farmer came to the door and said, "Good evening. What can I do for you?" And the man shouted, "Listen, Mister, you can take that jack of yours and shove it!"

STRAW-MAN ARGUMENT

Another diabolical way of "getting personal" is to attribute to your opponent a position she does not in fact hold and then attack her for this position. This is the so-called straw-man argument, and it is truly astonishing how often it slips by us undetected:

> SENATOR BARBARA BOXER: [to Condoleezza Rice in a hearing on the Iraq war] *Who pays the price? I'm not going to pay a personal price. My kids are too old and my grandchild is too young. You're not going to pay a particular price, as I understand it, with an immediate family. So who pays the price? The American military and their families. And I just want to bring us back to that fact.*

> SECRETARY OF STATE CONDOLEEZZA RICE: [after the hearing] *I thought it was okay to be single. I thought it was okay to not have children, and I thought you could still make good decisions on behalf of the country if you were single and didn't have children.*

Hello?? Condi?? Did anyone say it's not okay to be single or to not have children? Or that it's not okay for single, childless people to make decisions on behalf of the country?

Secretary Rice has ignored Senator Boxer's actual position and substituted a distorted version. She has created a "straw man," or in this case a "straw woman," because it is easier to attack a straw woman than it is to attack the real Senator Boxer and her argument about who pays the price for reckless decisions. The straw-man argument is so called because of the military's use, in days of yore, of scarecrows, created for the sole purpose of being stand-in targets in training exercises.

The senator was understandably flummoxed by the secretary of state's reaction. "What I was trying to do in this exchange was to find common ground with Condi Rice," Senator Boxer said. "My whole point was to focus on the military families who pay the price. . . . I'm saying, she's like me, we do not have families who are in the military."

A joke or satire can skewer a political position without being charged with stabbing a straw man because, well, it's just a joke. But consider this so-called satirical list of the Top Five Liberal Beliefs, found on an anonymous blog:

5. AIDS is spread by lack of funding.
4. Gender roles are artificial, but being gay is natural.
3. Businesses create oppression and governments create prosperity.
2. Self-esteem is more important than actually doing something to earn it.
1. The same government that can't deliver the mail should provide healthcare.

Isn't a winking straw man still a straw man?

Senator Kerry was another victim of the straw-man manufacturers. A prepared speech read, "I can't overstress the importance of a great education. Do you know where you end up if you don't study, if you aren't smart, if you're intellectually lazy? You end up *getting us stuck in a war in Iraq.* Just ask President Bush." Unfortunately, what he actually said when he delivered the speech was, "Education, if you make the most of it, you study hard, you do your homework and you make an effort to be smart, you can do well. And if you don't, *you get stuck in Iraq.*" Despite having been provided a copy of Kerry's actual prepared remarks, the spin-meisters knew a good straw man when they saw one. A statement released by House Majority Leader John A. Boehner included a picture that purported to show soldiers in the desert holding up a banner that read HALP US JON CARRY—WE R STUCK HEAR N IRAK. The clear implication was that Kerry thought our troops are all uneducated boobs.

Okay, it's hard to gin up much sympathy for a man who shoots himself in the foot, but our bet is that the Republicans knew full well that Kerry, a Yale graduate who served in Vietnam, did not intend to say that only the uneducated serve in the military. A straw man is a straw man even when the actual man helps you create it.

CONTEXTOMY

A subtle variation on the straw-man argument goes by the tongue-twisting name of contextomy, or yanking your victim's words out of context. It's a straw-man argument because it still attributes a position to an opponent that he or she does not, in fact, hold, but this time around it pulls that off by using the opponent's own words . . . just out of context.

Again, we, the audience, sometimes conspire in this trick because we are willing to believe that the victim would say just such a kooky thing—and the attacker often depends on that when craftily choosing an out-of-context quote:

The Pacific yew can be cut down and processed to produce a potent chemical, taxol, which offers some promise of curing certain forms of lung, breast and ovarian cancer in patients who would otherwise quickly die. It seems an easy choice— sacrifice the tree for a human life—until one learns that three trees must be destroyed for each patient treated.

— Vice President AL GORE, in his 1992 book *Earth in the Balance*

Three trees versus a human life, three trees versus the ability to prolong someone's life who is suffering from cancer? I would pick the individual, the person, the human being who is a cancer patient and suffering from that dreaded disease and say it is clear three trees are worth it. We can sacrifice three trees to save one human life. But the Vice President apparently does not think that is so clear.

— Representative DAVID MCINTOSH, in a 1999 speech in the House of Representatives referring to the above quote, as recorded in a column in the *Austin American-Statesman*

Contextomy alert! Here is the larger context of the Gore quote McIntosh used to accuse him of being a yew hugger:

Most of the [tree] species unique to the rain forests are in imminent danger, partly because there is no one to speak

*up for them. In contrast, consider the recent controversy
over the yew tree, a temperate forest species, one variety
of which now grows only in the Pacific Northwest.*

**The Pacific yew can be cut down and processed to produce
a potent chemical, taxol, which offers some promise of
curing certain forms of lung, breast, and ovarian cancer in
patients who would otherwise quickly die. It seems an easy
choice—sacrifice the tree for a human life—until one learns
that three trees must be destroyed for each patient treated,**
*that only specimens more than a hundred years old contain
the potent chemical in their bark, and that there are very
few of these yews remaining on earth. Suddenly we must
confront some very tough questions. How important are the
medical needs of future generations? Are those of us alive
today entitled to cut down all of those trees to extend the
lives of a few of us, even if it means that this unique form
of life will disappear forever, thus making it impossible to
save human lives in the future?*

In other words, Gore's disinclination to cut down yews
was not motivated by a fanatical pro-yew platform, but by his
worry that harvesting too many now would limit the supply
available to benefit cancer patients of future generations.

Political contextomists appear to have learned their trade
from their fellow spin-meisters in show biz. Who hasn't read
a rave blurb quoted in an ad for a movie or play and wondered
just what the whole quote said? Say K-Fed Knocked 'em
Dead! is clipped from a longer review that reads, "If K-Fed

knocked 'em dead at the Vegas nightclub last night, it would have been a coup de grace."

And here's one from a two-page advertisement in *The New York Times* for the revival of *A Chorus Line*, as credited to the paper's top reviewer, Ben Brantley: WHAT OCCURS SHORTLY AFTER 8 P.M. AT THE SCHOENFELD THEATRE . . . FEELS SO FRESH THAT YOU STOP TO CATCH YOUR BREATH.

In fact, we didn't catch our breath until we went back to Brantley's full review, several degrees south of a rave, in which he wrote the following:

> **What occurs shortly after 8 p.m. at the Gerald Schoenfeld Theater,** where the otherwise pedestrian new revival of *A Chorus Line* opened last night, is a sort of time bending that Einstein would have trouble explaining. Light, music and a mass of bodies in motion combine to allow you to exist both in 1975, when this musical was first staged, and 2006. This *is* what *A Chorus Line* was when I saw it 31 years ago, and yet it **feels so fresh that you stop to catch your breath**. . . . Watching the show, directed by Bob Avian, is like drinking from a pitcher of draft beer: You never repeat the tang or sting of that first swig. . . . [I]n providing us with an archivally and anatomically correct reproduction of a landmark show, its creators neglected to restore its central nervous system and, most important, its throbbing heart.

In other words, yews had to be there.

* *

GOD IS MY COPILOT

Some of the less subtle politicians down through the ages (think Attila the Hun or Vlad the Impaler and their ilk, who don't cry over spilled blood) had their own variation on "So's your mother." It might have been called "So's my father." Their *ad hominem* argument was basically, "It's so, just because Dad says it's so." The Dad in question is, of course, their Heavenly Father.

> *I am the Flail of God. If you had not committed great sins,*
> *God would not have sent a punishment like me upon you.*
> — GENGHIS KHAN (1162–1227)

It's kind of refreshing to hear an honest politician speak his mind, isn't it? You could always count on G. Khan to tell it the way he saw it.

But Genghis is doing way more than that in this statement: He is addressing the age-old theological conundrum of how a good and just God could possibly allow so much dreadfulness to happen on his grand creation, Earth. His answer: *"God knows if you've been bad or good, so if you haven't been good, for goodness' sake, he (and I) are simply going to make you pay for it, big-time. This is the way the Lord keeps Good in the driver's seat. It works for him, not to mention me, the Flail of God."*

Implicit in Genghis's line of thinking is that he has the inside track to God's thinking and motives, that he is God's personal henchman—in short, *Deus est auriga meus* ("God

"But how do you know for sure you've got power unless you abuse it?"

is my charioteer"). Needless to mention, the Khan was and is not alone in this belief: God under various monikers still speaks directly to world figures, often advising them to commit murder in his name.

When asked if he had discussed the invasion of Iraq with his father, former president George H. W. Bush, George W. Bush replied, "You know, he is the wrong father to appeal to in terms of strength. There is a higher father that I appeal to."

In some families this might be seen as disrespecting one's elders, but that aside, Bush Jr.'s riposte once again raises the question of how the Higher Father chooses his deputies out of all those who seek the position. Is it arbitrary? A personal choice? Perhaps this story sheds some light on the process:

A lame man in rags crawls down the aisle of a church to the altar, raises his eyes to the heavens and cries out, "Lord, why have you chosen me for all these afflictions?"

Suddenly, a sphere of blinding light appears just above him in the sanctuary and a thunderous voice intones, "I don't know, Charlie, there's just something about you that pisses me off."

But granting Genghis his insider status, let's consider his proposition. He is invoking logic's basic formulation, the if/then proposition. So let's try spinning Mr. Khan's statement around, using the *valid* logical gambit called denying the consequent. From "*If* you had not committed great sins, [*then*] God would not have sent a punishment like me upon you," we can deduce, "*If* God sent a punishment like me upon you, *then* you must have committed great sins." And therein lies the beauty of this gambit: It is unassailable—*there is no evidence that will disprove it!* Whatever I do to you is your own fault!

Like Groucho Marx, who said, "I wouldn't belong to any club that would have me as a member," Mr. K. is implying he would not want to be part of any tribe that has him as a flail.

But do we hear Genghis protesting? *"Wait a minute! You're making it sound like I'm an arbitrary dispenser of punishment, that I do whatever I like and then justify it by saying that whatever I do is okay because it is I who did it. Give me some bloody credit here! You're confusing me with that upcoming barbarian, Louis XIV, who said, 'It is legal because I wish it.' On the contrary, with Divine Flailhood comes responsibility. I wouldn't do anything ungodly to you, and therefore, if I punished you, you must have had it coming."*

It may sound absurd to attribute such refined sentiments and nuanced arguments to Genghis Khan, but something like that underlies the pope's claim to infallibility and perhaps even W's war on evildoers—although we don't pretend to know how W's mind works. It may not be quite *Deus est auriga meus*, but it does assume a unique and unarguable ability to interpret God's will.

"Try to think of the Lord as a 24-hour video surveillance system gathering pictures for the ultimate 'Crimewatch.'"

"GOD MADE ME DO IT!" LORE

The use of "God made me do it"—as both a principle of action and an excuse for it—declined after Genghis, replaced by "the devil made me do it." In both cases, personal moral responsibility was nullified, so it was just a hop, skip, and jump to "My unconscious drives made me do it," a.k.a. the insanity defense.

What is striking about all three Über-Motivators is that they almost exclusively make us do criminal acts. As one comedian quipped, "Have you ever heard anyone cry, 'God made me trim the hedges!'"

PROJECTION

Okay, time to check in with a "So's your mother" quiz. Who, in 1941, said the following words, and about whom was he speaking?

> For over five years this man has been chasing around Europe like a madman in search of something he could set on fire. Unfortunately, he again and again finds hirelings who open the gates of their country to this international incendiary.

Most reasonable quizees would guess that the speaker was some wise politician like Winston Churchill, referring to Adolf Hitler. And they would have it exactly wrong. It was Hitler referring to Churchill!

Was Hitler simply being wily and consciously perverse by making this pronouncement, or was there some other mechanism at work here? Our guess is the latter, although God knows it was perverse too. But before we get into this, a disclaimer: Volumes have been written about the inner workings of Hitler's mind, and we know that psychoanalytic interpretations are, at best, speculative. But in this case the utter counterintuitiveness of the Führer's pronouncement begs for some kind of explanation, unprovable as it may be.

In his assertion about Winston, Adolf appears to have been in the thrall of a psychological mechanism known as projection. According to Freud, projection occurs when one is threatened by or afraid of one's own impulses and consequently attributes those impulses to someone else. For example, a client undergoing psychoanalysis may insist to the therapist that he knows the therapist wants to coldcock him, when in fact it is the client who unconsciously longs to whap the therapist.

A classic gag captures this defense mechanism perfectly:

SHRINK: When I show you this triangle, what's the first thing that comes into your mind?

PATIENT: Two men and a woman going at it on a water bed.

SHRINK: How about when I show you this circle?

PATIENT: Some girl-on-girl action in the locker room shower.

SHRINK: And this square?

PATIENT: A woman taking on three men in the backseat of a Volvo.

SHRINK: Okay, I've arrived at my diagnosis. You're obsessed with sex.

PATIENT: Me? You're the one with the dirty-picture collection!

But the most significant question is, Why would some ordinary person, or at least some ordinary 1940s German, be taken in by such a transparent transposition of who the genuine bad guy is?

The answer lies in the passionate fervor of the speaker of these words. He is so vehement, so confident, so frankly horrified by what he sees as their collective enemy that it is hard not to believe he is speaking the truth. Passion and fervor are the hallmarks of effective rhetoric. And in the case of an orator who is suffering from projection, he is characteristically filled with passion and fervor. Psychoanalytically, he has transferred his self-loathing into the loathing of someone else, and as we all know, self-loathing is about as passionate and fervid as any kind of loathing gets.

Wars and elections seem to trigger the psychopathology of projection. When one party (whom we shall call party A, for purposes of identification) grants huge tax cuts, mainly to the superrich, and the opposing party (here called party B) points out the unfairness of this measure, how does party A respond? By passionately and fervently crying, "Party B is igniting class warfare!"

* *

ARGUMENTUM AD VERECUNDIAM
(APPEAL TO AUTHORITY)

There are several approaches to misleading by getting personal that do not involve getting nasty. Happily, we don't come away from these arguments feeling sullied. Unhappily, we still come away from these arguments with highly questionable ideas. Consider the appeal to authority:

> *These past couple of weeks, Sox fans trusted me when it was my turn on the mound. Now you can trust me on this: President Bush is the right leader for our country.*
>
> — Boston Red Sox pitcher CURT SCHILLING

> *I believe that John Kerry honors these ideals. He has lived their history over the past 50 years and formed an adult view of America and its people.*
>
> — Singer/songwriter BRUCE SPRINGSTEEN

The appeal to authority attempts to bolster an argument by citing support from people regarded as authoritative and prestigious. And who is more prestigious in the U.S.A. than ballplayers and rock stars?

The appeal to authority is obviously not fallacious in and of itself. Citing Einstein to back up your opinion on the space-time continuum, as we often do, is actually a cool move and one that has worked well for us over the years. That's why some authorities on informal logic prefer to call this fallacy the appeal to *questionable* authority. Like, why should

Schilling's expertise with a fastball give him any cachet as a political commentator?

When Hillary Clinton said, in 1992, "You know, I'm not sitting here, some little woman standing by my man like Tammy Wynette," the press *appropriately* turned to an expert—not on politics, but on both standin' by one's man and on being Tammy Wynette—namely, Tammy Wynette. (Her response: "Well, what *was* she doin', then?")

The case of the Dixie Chicks is more instructive. When the Chicks expressed their displeasure at being from the same state as the president, the country music public questioned their expertise. The fan who yelled, "Shut up and sing!" was in effect saying, "Y'all don't know squat about war or politics." Interestingly, the liberal wing of the National Academy of Recording Arts and Sciences tried to restore the Chicks' legitimacy as political pundits—by heaping as many Grammys on them as possible.

But the biggest problem with the argument from authority is that anyone can just keep looking for an authority until they find one who says what they want said:

A man wonders if having sex on the Sabbath is a sin, because he is not sure if sex is work or play. So he goes to a priest and asks his opinion.

After consulting church teachings, the priest says, "My son, after an exhaustive search, I have concluded that sex is work and is therefore contrary to the commandment to rest from your labor on the Sabbath."

But the man thinks, *Is a celibate priest really the best authority*

★ ★

on sex? So he goes to see a married minister. The minister consults the Bible and reaches the same conclusion: Sex is work and therefore not permitted on the Sabbath.

Not pleased with the reply, the man turns to another authority: a rabbi. The rabbi ponders the question briefly and says, "My son, sex is definitely play."

The delighted man replies, "Rabbi, that's wonderful news, but, tell me, how can you be so sure when so many others tell me sex is work?"

The rabbi answers, "If sex were work, my wife would have the maid do it."

GUILTY WITH EXPLANATION

Scores of politicians have used another of the less toxic getting-personal gambits, guilty with explanation, an attempt to garner sympathetic understanding by acknowledging a mistake while also trying to explain it away. It's kind of like saying, "I'm sorry, but actually I don't have anything to be sorry about." Neat trick.

Like when, after repeatedly insisting that Secretary of Defense Donald Rumsfeld would "remain with me until the end of my presidency," President George W. Bush announced that he was letting Rumsfeld go one day after the 2006 midterm elections were won by the Democrats:

REPORTER: *Last week you told us Secretary Rumsfeld would be staying on. Why is the timing right now for this, and how much does it have to do with the election results?*

BUSH: *You . . . asked me the question one week before the campaign . . . and my answer was, they're going to stay on. And the reason why is **I did not want to inject a major decision in the final days of the campaign. The only way to answer that question, and get it on to another question, was to give you that answer.***

When the guilty with explanation ruse is invoked, some explanations work better than others. In the case at hand, the president had been caught in an obvious inconsistency: One week he says he'll *never* let Rumsfeld go, the next he says the time has come for a new man for a new course—so bye-bye, Rummy. Bush might have simply admitted that circumstances had unexpectedly prompted him to change his mind, either about firing Rumsfeld or about the timing of the announcement. But the Decider-in-Chief has a consistent aversion to admitting inconsistencies. So instead he offered an explanation that he apparently thought would appeal to our sympathetic understanding. He suggested, in effect, that it would have been unfair and improper to fire Rumsfeld (or to make public his decision to do so) before the election, because that could have influenced its results, a noble-sounding excuse if we've ever heard one.

But one test of the effectiveness of the guilty with explanation maneuver is the believability of the explanation. Most observers believe that, given Rumsfeld's stunning unpopularity among the voting public, the most probable effect of firing Rumsfeld *before* the election would have been to garner more votes for Republicans. Wow! That makes the president's explanation sound even more sympathetic by demonstrating just how fair-minded he was being. But believable? No way. Most observers also think that if the Republicans had kept their congressional majorities in the election, Rummy would have kept his job.

There's an old farmer joke that shows the guilty with explanation ploy meeting the believability test head-on. Of course, the joke does run on, as farmer jokes will:

A farmer named Clyde had a car accident. In court, the trucking company's fancy hotshot lawyer questioned Clyde: "Didn't you say, at the scene of the accident, 'I'm fine'?" demanded the lawyer.

Clyde responded, "Well, I'll tell you what happened. I had just loaded my favorite cow, Bessie, into the—"

"I didn't ask for any details," the lawyer interrupted. "Just answer the question. Did you not say, at the scene of the accident, 'I'm fine'?"

Clyde responded, "Well, I had just got Bessie into the trailer and I was driving down the road—"

The lawyer interrupted again and addressed the judge: "Your Honor, I am trying to establish the fact that, at the scene of the accident, this man told the highway patrolman that he was just fine. Now, several weeks after the accident, he is trying to sue my client. I believe he is a fraud. Please tell him to simply answer the question."

By this time, the judge was rather interested in Clyde's answer and said to the lawyer, "I'd like to hear what he has to say about his favorite cow, Bessie."

Clyde thanked the judge and proceeded. "Well, as I was saying, I had just loaded Bessie, my favorite cow, into the trailer and was driving her down the highway, when this huge semitrailer ran the stop sign and smacked my truck right in the side. I was thrown into one ditch, and Bessie was thrown into the other. I was hurting real bad and didn't want to move. However, I could hear old Bessie moaning and groaning. I knew she was in terrible shape just by her groans. Shortly after the accident a highway patrolman came on the scene. He could hear Bessie moaning and groaning, so he went over to her. After he looked at her and saw her fatal condition, he took out his gun and shot her between the eyes.

"Then the patrolman came across the road, gun still in hand, looked at me, and asked, 'How are you feeling?'

"Now what the hell would you say?"

KAIROS (GOOD TIMING)

Apologizing is always tricky for politicians: They have to appear humble yet strong, caring yet dignified, responsible yet inculpable. But combining opposites has never been a problem for skilled politicos. And, like master comedians, they know timing is everything.

> *[We regret] extermination, termination, forced removal and relocation, the outlawing of traditional religions, and the destruction of sacred places.*
>
> — Bill submitted by Representative JO ANN DAVIS, apologizing for the United States' treatment of Native Americans

Surely every American knows that slavery was wrong, and we paid a terrible price for [it], and that we had to keep repairing that. And just to say that it's wrong and that we are sorry about it is not a bad thing.

— President BILL CLINTON, *sort of* apologizing for slavery

[We have enacted] a law calling for restitution and offering [you] a sincere apology.

— President GEORGE H. W. BUSH, apologizing for the internment of Japanese Americans during World War II

I wish you'd have given me this written question ahead of time so I could plan for it. John, I'm sure historians will look back and say, gosh, he could've done it better this way or that way. You know, I just—I'm sure something will pop into my head here in the midst of this press conference, with all the pressure of trying to come up with an answer, but it hasn't yet.

— President GEORGE W. BUSH, *not* apologizing for any mistakes made since 9/11

Well, I have said, and I will repeat it, that knowing what I know now, I never would have voted for it.

— Senator HILLARY CLINTON, *not* apologizing for her vote to authorize the war, in response to a challenge from a New Hampshire voter: "I want to know if right here, right now, once and for all and without nuance, you can say that war authorization was a mistake."

Mistakes were made.

— President RICHARD NIXON, *not* apologizing for Watergate;
also, Attorney General ALBERTO GONZALES, *not* apologizing
for the firing of eight federal prosecutors

First, a word about *kairos*, a key term in Aristotle's treatise
on rhetoric. It is one of those multiple-meaning terms that
drive translators up the wall, but a list of its most frequent
connotations includes "timing," "right timing," "oppor-
tunistic timing," *eukairos* ("good timing"), and *kakakairos*
("bad timing").

These days, *kairos* is most frequently bandied about with
respect to the rapid response of candidates and government
agencies to news stories and allegations they want to "correct."
Eukairos has a new urgency in the twenty-four-hour news
cycle—the faster the comeback, the better. The White House
even has a job title called "White House director of rapid
response," and that's not for missile attacks; it's for verbal
attacks.

But there is an exception to the faster-is-better rule that
would make Aristotle's head spin like a celestial sphere: *apologizing*. When it comes to heartfelt apologies, *slower* is far better. In fact, a good rule of thumb for contemporary politicians
is that apologies for anything that happened before 1950 are
probably okay, but pre–Civil War is better, and pre-Federalist
is better yet.

That's why we have to cut Presidents Bush and Nixon and
Senator Clinton some slack here. It's tough to apologize for

something that happened within human memory, because it comes dangerously close to actually taking personal responsibility.

It's like the cabbie who picked up the nun:

A nun gets into a cab and notices that the young cab driver is staring at her in the rearview mirror. She asks him why he's staring, and he says, "I have a question to ask you, but I don't want to offend you."

She answers, "My son, you cannot offend me. When you're as old as I am and have been a nun as long as I have, you get a chance to see and hear just about everything. I'm sure that there's nothing you could say or ask that I would find offensive."

"Well," he says, "I've always had a fantasy of kissing a nun."

She replies, "Well, that's perfectly understandable. I may be able to help you with that, but only if you're single and Catholic."

The cab driver cries out, "Yes! I'm single and Catholic!"

"Okay," the nun says. "Pull into the next alley."

There, he kisses the nun passionately, but when they get back on the road, the cab driver begins to sob.

"My dear child," says the nun. "Why are you crying?"

"Sister, it is very painful to have to apologize to you for something I did only moments ago, but I must ask your forgiveness. I have sinned. I lied, and I must confess. I'm married and I'm a Baptist."

"Oh, don't worry about it, hon," the nun answers. "My name is Eric, and I'm on my way to a Halloween party."

*"Hi, hon. Guess who's going to be on national television
apologizing to the American public."*

QUI DICIT (WHO SAYS SO?)

Perhaps the purest example of the rhetorical effect of getting personal is the principle of *qui dicit?* ("who says so?"). It turns out that some people are *not* culturally permitted to say certain things that other people *are* permitted to say. Just ask Don Imus, who, at least at the time he uttered his infamous words "nappy-headed hos," was neither an African American nor a rapper. Or consider the case of Mayor Ray Nagin, who was running for reelection at the time of this statement:

> *I don't care what people are saying Uptown or wherever they are. **This city will be chocolate at the end of the day.** This city will be a majority African-American city. It's the way God wants it to be.*
> — New Orleans mayor RAY NAGIN, on the rebuilding of his city after Hurricane Katrina

> *What I'm hearing, which is sort of scary, is they all want to stay in Texas. Everyone is so overwhelmed by the hospitality. And so many of the people in the arena here, you know, were **underprivileged anyway, so this is working very well for them.***
> First Mother and former first lady BARBARA BUSH, on Katrina victims temporarily housed in Houston's Astrodome

Here we have another from the *hominem* variations, arguments whose power and rectitude are in some ways dependent on *who* says them and, often, *how* and *to whom*.

In *qui dicit?* we discover that for person A to say X to person A types is perfectly okay, but for person A to say X to persons of type B is way bad, an improper and unfair form of discourse. Further, for person B to say X to *absolutely anybody* is *verboten*. For example, for a Jew to tell to another Jew a joke that depends on Jewish stereotypes for its punch is usually permissible, but for that Jew to tell the same joke to a Gentile would be considered bad form. More tellingly, for any Gentile to tell the very same joke to anyone, Jew or Gentile, would immediately open that Gentile to charges of anti-Semitism. On the face of it, that doesn't seem fair, but that's *homines* for you.

Another example—the use of the n-word—gets closer to Mayor Nagin's infamous utterance. In the African-American scholar Randall Kennedy's provocative book *Nigger: The Strange Career of a Troublesome Word*, the author points out that for many contemporary blacks the word can be used as a term of endearment for one another, while obviously the same is not the case for a white addressing a black. Mayor Nagin is an African American who, in his use of the Hershey word, *was addressing the general public*. For that reason, New Orleans residents, black and white, took him to task. Most of Nagin's critics, rather than accusing him of using racist language, accused him of being divisive at a time when the city needed to come together. But context is everything, and if Nagin had confined his cocoa-product metaphor to, say, the pulpit of a black church (with no microphones or reporters present), it may have been greeted with warm laughter.

Of course, some commentators are of the opinion that Nagin knew exactly what he was saying, and to whom—black voters. The argument is that although these voters may have publicly objected to the supposedly racist term, privately it gave them a sense of community. By the way, he won his reelection handily.

There is something about a tragedy like Katrina that brings class and race insensitivity—not to mention warfare—to the surface. Barbara Bush's comment about the poor folk never having had it better than when living in the Astrodome set loose a tempest. She was accused of being an insensitive, patronizing elitist. It's certainly hard to argue with that, but if some Astrodome residents had told a CNN reporter that they'd never slept in an air-conditioned place before and it was a real treat, the story probably wouldn't have lasted beyond a single news cycle.

PART III

The Fancy Footwork Strategy

Misleading with Informal Fallacies

Alas, we have to revisit the question of whether politicos make intricate logical errors on purpose or because they really don't know any better. After thinking long and hard, we've decided to give them the benefit of the doubt: We believe they would rather be called devious than dense.

CUM HOC ERGO PROPTER HOC
(WITH THIS, THEREFORE BECAUSE OF THIS)

A whole bunch of these logical flimflams happen around the notion of cause and effect. The first of these, originally described by Aristotle, is known as "with this, therefore because of this." But it sounds better in Latin, so it's usually called *cum hoc ergo propter hoc*, despite the fact that Aristotle spoke Greek. Don't ask.

Here's an example:

* *

> *The highest increases in the rate of child poverty in*
> *recent years have occurred in those states which pay the*
> *highest welfare benefits. The lowest increases—or actual*
> *decreases—in child poverty have occurred in states which*
> *restrain the level of AFDC payments.*

— Conservative political advocate GARY BAUER, president of the
   Family Research Council and a senior vice president of Focus
   on the Family, arguing that welfare causes child poverty

In this case, Mr. Bauer makes the fundamental mistake of disregarding the possibility of a third factor, such as the general economic status of the states where welfare and child poverty fluctuate. As it turns out, the median income declined or was flat in the ten states where welfare costs and child poverty went up, while income rose substantially in nine of the ten states where welfare payments and poverty escalated least. In other words, economic decline may have caused an increase in both welfare and child poverty. We're sure Mr. Bauer regrets his faulty reasoning on behalf of families everywhere.

But he is not alone in committing the fallacy *cum hoc ergo propter hoc*. Consider President Bush's oft-repeated sentiment that the war in Iraq is preventing attacks on our country, as illustrated in this example:

> *The commander in charge of coalition forces in Iraq—who*
> *is also senior Commander at this base—General John*
> *Vines, put it well the other day. He said: "We either deal*

*with terrorism and this extremism abroad, or we deal with
it when it comes to us."*
— President GEORGE W. BUSH, June 2005

Exactly how does that work? Is it that the terrorists are
too busy? Surely Al-Qaeda could free up nineteen men again
if they thought they could get away with it. In any case, it's
hardly a sure bet that it's the war in Iraq that has prevented us
from being attacked at home. It's like a guy painting his house
pink to ward off dragons. Call him nuts and he points to his
success rate.

CAUSE AND DEFECT

Melvin was dying. He was old, very old. He had seen
much suffering in his life. Trudy, his wife, was seated on
the edge of the bed, wiping his brow. They had lived
together for more than seventy years.

"Tell me, Trudy, do you remember the Depression
years when we barely had enough to get by?" he asked her.

"Of course I remember. I was with you through all
that," Trudy answered.

"Do you remember the lean years after the war,
when I was working two jobs and going to school?"

"Of course. I was with you then too, my love."

"Were you with me when I lost my job?"

"Of course, my love, I've always been with you. Always."

* *

Melvin was silent for a moment. Then he looked at his loving wife. "You see, Trudy, I think you were bad luck."

POST HOC ERGO PROPTER HOC
(AFTER THIS, THEREFORE BECAUSE OF THIS)

A cousin of *cum hoc ergo propter hoc* is *post hoc ergo propter hoc*. You can tell they're related because they have the same last name. *Post hoc* arguments assume that B is caused by A because B came *after* A.

One area where *PHEPH* trickery frequently occurs is in the realm of statistics, namely positing numerical data of one phenomenon as the *cause* of another phenomenon also expressed as numerical data. The beauty part of this technique is that we get bamboozled by the impressive precision of the numbers, so much so that we may neglect to realize that one set of numbers is actually unrelated to the other set:

> *The 10 states with the lowest per pupil spending included four—North Dakota, South Dakota, Tennessee, Utah— among the 10 states with the top SAT scores. Only one of the 10 states with the highest per pupil expenditures— Wisconsin—was among the 10 states with the highest SAT scores. New Jersey has the highest per pupil expenditures, an astonishing $10,561, which teachers' unions elsewhere try to use as a negotiating benchmark. New Jersey's rank regarding SAT scores? Thirty-ninth. . . . The fact that the quality of schools . . . [fails to correlate]*

*with education appropriations will have no effect on
the teacher unions' insistence that money is the crucial
variable. The public education lobby's crumbling last line
of defense is the miseducation of the public.*

—Conservative political commentator GEORGE WILL

   (*Washington Post*, September 12, 1993)

Before we address Commentator Will's *post hoc* reasoning, we have a few words we would like to throw out there—actually, other people's words:

*There are three kinds of lies: lies, damned lies,
and statistics.*

— BENJAMIN DISRAELI, petulant British prime minister

79.48% of all statistics are made up on the spot.

— JOHN PAULOS, professor of mathematics

*One out of every four people is suffering from some form
of mental illness. Check three friends. If they're OK, then
it's you.*

— RITA MAE BROWN, feminist wit

Okay, just one more, we promise:

*Statistics: The only science that enables different experts
using the same figures to draw different conclusions.*

— EVAN ESAR, prolific epigramologist

Our point is a fairly common one: It is easy to derive a false conclusion from statistical data (this is sometimes known as "lying with statistics"). Perhaps less well known is that the specific fallacy involved in getting to these false conclusions is the old *post hoc ergo propter hoc*. A piece of statistical information about phenomenon A is posited as the cause of phenomenon B (also statistically documented) that comes after it. Or, in Mr. Will's case, the causative effect that he thinks *should have been* demonstrated by the earlier event is not demonstrated. The problem, of course, is that the two phenomena may be totally unrelated. Or, as in the case of Mr. Will's thesis, the statistics employed may be incomplete—they do not tell the whole story because they omit data relevant to the proposed cause-and-effect relationship.

In the *Journal of Statistics Education*, Deborah Lynn Guber points out that a crucial factor Mr. Will ignores in his analysis is participation rates: the percentage of students in each state who *actually take the SAT*. It turns out that in North Dakota, state colleges require the ACT rather than the SAT, so only 5 percent of North Dakota students take the SAT. It is fair to say that among that 5 percent are a large number of students who want to go to prestigious out-of-state schools (that *do* require the SAT) and who, because of their proven academic abilities, think they have a shot at it. In New Jersey, by comparison, 79 percent of students take the SAT—certainly a more representative cross-section of the entire population of high school graduates. So the SAT scores of the brightest ND students are being compared to the SAT scores of more typical NJ students.

*"That's the gist of what I want to say.
Now get me some statistics to base it on."*

This is like comparing the four Jamaican bobsledders in the 1988 Olympics to a cross-section of American bobsledders, finding that the Jamaicans are *on average* superior, and concluding that being born in Jamaica makes for being a better bobsledder.

Interestingly, when Mr. Will concludes that there's no correlation between SAT scores (or "quality of schools"—Will blithely acts as if the two are synonymous) and education appropriations, it is a rather restrained judgment that he draws. He might have made a case, albeit a fallacious one, that there's a *negative correlation*! After all, four of the states with the lowest spending per pupil rank among the highest in SAT scores, while the state with the highest spending per pupil ranked thirty-ninth in SAT scores. Maybe Will realized that by this logic, it could be argued that the best way to produce the highest SAT scores would be to defund education completely.

A CASUALTY OF CASUAL CAUSALITY

Confusing an intermediate cause for a primary cause can sometimes make you wish you'd gotten a second opinion.

So this guy goes to his doctor and complains that he's been having blinding headaches for years now and nothing helps. The doc gives him a thorough examination, sits him down, and tells him that he has a rare disorder: The headaches are a result of his testicles pressing against the base of his spine. The only cure is surgical castration.

The guy thinks about his options for weeks and finally concludes that the headaches are unbearable, so he decides to get the operation.

Afterward, he is understandably depressed, if headache-free. He decides to cheer himself up by buying some new clothes, and goes to a men's shop.

"I want a pin-striped suit," he tells the old salesman.

The salesman takes one look at him and says, "Hmm, 42 long, 33 on the inseam."

"On the button," the guy says. "How'd you do that?"

"Sonny, when you've been in this business as long as I have, you get a second sense for these things."

The guy asks for a dress shirt to go with the suit, and the salesman says, "Yup, 16½ in the neck, 34 in the sleeve."

"Amazing!" the guy says, starting to feel cheered up by the salesman. "Hey, while I'm here, I'll get some briefs too."

"Size 36!" the salesman says.

"Nope, you're wrong this time," the guy says. "I wear a 34."

"Sonny," the salesman says. "You don't want a 34—that'd press your balls against the base of your spine and give you one hell of a headache!"

* *

Here's another bit of *post hoc* gobbledygook perpetrated by a couple of political "scientists" (quotation marks ours):

> *We test the **effects** of a popular televised source of political humor for young Americans:* The Daily Show with Jon Stewart. ***We find that participants exposed to jokes about George W. Bush and John Kerry on* The Daily Show *tended to rate both candidates more negatively,*** *even when controlling for partisanship and other demographic variables.* ***Moreover, we find that viewers exhibit more cynicism toward the electoral system and the news media at large.***
>
> — JODY BAUMGARTNER and JONATHAN MORRIS, researchers and assistant professors in the Political Science Department at East Carolina University, in "*The Daily Show* Effect: Candidate Evaluations, Efficacy, and American Youth" (*American Politics Research*, an academic journal)

Thanks, Jody and Jon. We knew there was something subversive about *The Daily Show*; we just couldn't put our fingers on it. But on behalf of all the other nonacademics out there, let's review your wacky logic:

1. Folks who watch *The Daily Show* tend to be more cynical than, say, folks who watch Katie Couric.
2. Therefore, *The Daily Show* must *cause* its viewers to *become* more cynical.

Oops! What we have here is another stunning example of *post hoc ergo propter hoc.* The lure of "after this, therefore because of this" is the fact that when A causes B, B obviously has to come after A. It's a *necessary condition* of causality that the presumed effect come after the presumed cause. But it's not a *sufficient condition*. There may be other causes, totally unrelated to A, at work.

FREAKOLOGIC

Another dazzling example of the fallacy *post hoc ergo propter hoc* is supplied by none other than that mega-bestseller *Freakonomics*. (Granted, the cover of the book advises the reader "Prepare to be dazzled," but it does not go on to say "with faulty logic.") The most-talked-about cause-and-effect phenomenon put forward by one of the authors, University of Chicago economist Steven Levitt, is his contention that the legalization of abortion by the *Roe v. Wade* decision caused—some twelve to seventeen years later—a drastic reduction in the crime rate. Levitt argues that the elimination of unwanted children, mostly from poor families, reduced the number of potential criminals, reasoning that unwanted children are more likely to become troubled adolescents, prone to crime and drug use, than are wanted children.

The thesis's political incorrectness aside (rarely a test of logic, in any event), Levitt's argument fails the sufficient condition test because it doesn't take into consideration other probable causes of the reduction in the crime rate during that same period (the 1980s and

1990s)—for example, the fact that the crack wave sub-sided precipitously at the time, as a result of a reduced supply of the drug.[iii]

Drawing cause-and-effect conclusions in the realm of social and cultural shifts is always a tricky business, because there are so many factors that can come into play. Consider the sociologist who discovers that every time there's a rice crop failure in Indonesia, there's a subsequent increase in the number of people in Brooklyn who lose their gloves. (Well, actually, that sociologist probably has a bestseller on his hands.)

To prove that a cause-and-effect relationship exists between watching Jon Stewart make fun of politicians and *becoming cynical* about the political process, profs Baumgartner and Morris would first have to examine a reasonable sample of people *before* they'd ever watched the show to see how cynical they were to begin with. Then they would have to test them for cynicism *after* they started watching Stewart regularly. Because it might just turn out—we're only guessing here—that the people who decide to watch *The Daily Show* do so because they were cynical to begin with. And the root cause of that cynicism might have been—we're going out on a limb here—watching actual politicians bullshit on Katie Couric's show.

There is no end of *post hoc ergo propter hoc* jokes that illustrate this fallacy, but this one's a favorite:

A thirty-something Gentile gentleman falls in love with a Jewish girl and proposes to her. She says that in order to marry her, he will have to get circumcised. So the GG goes to a Jewish male friend and asks if circumcision has any negative side effects.

The Jewish guy says, "Well, I was only eight weeks old when I had mine, so I can't remember if it was painful. But I do know that afterwards I couldn't walk for a year!"

Incidentally, we have done a survey ourselves, and we've discovered that an effect of reading *American Politics Research* is consuming a diet high in saturated fats.

Some may question whether there is anything cynical about Jon Stewart in the first place. For those, we offer a few choice Stewart lines:

Despite his infirmities, Strom Thurmond showed up to work every day and did not miss a Senate vote in his final year, though no one is sure if a shouted "Bingo!" counted as a yea or a nay.

I celebrated Thanksgiving in an old-fashioned way. I invited everyone in my neighborhood to my house, we had an enormous feast, and then I killed them and took their land.

If the events of September 11, 2001, have proven anything, it's that the terrorists can attack us, but they can't take away what makes us American—our freedom, our liberty, our civil rights. No, only Attorney General John Ashcroft can do that.

Cynical? We leave it to your judgment.

*   *

Cum hoc and *post hoc* arguments owe much of their appeal to our fanciful/poetic sides, which, from a strict philosopher's point of view, are our pudding-headed sides. Such forms of loosey-goosey thinking have been popularized by the myth known as the butterfly effect, which alleges that a single butterfly's wings can generate minute atmospheric changes that, through a chain of cause-and-effect events, ultimately create a tornado. Actually, non-pudding-headed physicists who subscribe to chaos theory give some credence to the butterfly effect, calling it "sensitive dependence on initial conditions," which doesn't sound half as appealing as the butterfly moniker.

But in popular culture, the butterfly effect usually refers to If-I-Had-It-All-to-Do-Over-Again-and-Chose-Option-B-Instead-of-Option-A-How-Different-My-Life-Would-Be! Like in the classic movie *It's a Wonderful Life* or the recent one titled, well, *The Butterfly Effect*. Yet in these scenarios, only the heroes' lives change—not the entire universe, as is the case in chaos theory.

In any event, the butterfly effect's major effect on our thinking is to loosen our standards for what counts as a provable cause of an event. Like, hey, maybe an IED in Baghdad creates an atmospheric condition that causes a windstorm that makes a terrorist in Dubai miss his plane for New York. Now there's a reason to stay in Iraq!

Cause-and-effect errors are just the tip of the iceberg of illogical propositions, so we need to take measures to steer clear of them, like a little deep-sea diving.

Unprovable Premise

OMG ("Oh my God!")! Are those the Founding Fathers we see under here?

> **We hold these truths to be self-evident**, *that all men are created equal, that they are endowed by their Creator with certain unalienable Rights, that among these are Life, Liberty, and the pursuit of Happiness.*
> — THOMAS JEFFERSON ET AL, the Declaration of Independence

We locked our doors prior to deconstructing this one. And after that, we paused to pledge our allegiance to the flag of the United States of America. We would think our allegiance would be self-evident, but you can't be too careful these days.

In fact, it's that "self-evident" business in the D of I that deserves scrutiny. The clear implication of the term is that this self-evidence is evident to *everyone* who is paying attention. But you don't need to be an epistemologist to realize that one person's "self-evident" is another person's "huh??" Our local shaman finds it self-evident that there are multicolored pixies fluttering around our heads. We are willing to accept that said pixies are evident to *his* self; they just don't happen to be evident to *ours*. And so for him to say, for example, that, because of these self-evident pixies, it is clear that we need to wear lampshades on our heads . . . well, the inference lacks a certain certainty. He is starting from a questionable and certainly unprovable premise, which throws all that is implied by his premise into doubt.

The term *self-evident* is generally reserved for logical and mathematical constructions, like 2 + 2 = 4. It can even be stretched to include statements like "This coat is red"—although if no one else viewing the coat thinks it's red, we even have to question that (see "multicolored pixies"). But although we definitely hold Life, Liberty, and the pursuit of Happiness in the highest esteem and may even be willing to risk our lives for these values, we can hardly call them self-evident in any strict sense. To pick a random example, King George III didn't find these values self-evident, at least not for the colonial riffraff.

Jefferson, as we know, uses these allegedly self-evident rights, along with a list of the ways in which King George has violated them, to conclude that revolution is justified. The shakiness of the premise—that the rights are self-evident—doesn't mean, of course, that revolution isn't justified. You can get a true conclusion arguing from a false or questionable premise. If our local shaman concluded from the existence of pixies that $E = mc^2$, that equation would still be true on its own merits. In other words (FBI, please take note), we're not arguing against the legitimacy of the American Revolution.

Jefferson's inspiration for the Declaration of Independence came from the British philosopher John Locke, who wrote in his *Two Treatises of Government* that "life, liberty, *health, and property*" (emphasis ours) were God-given rights that a just government should accord its citizens. Locke also argued that owning property is the key to happiness. Perhaps Jefferson's switch to "life, liberty, and the *pursuit of happiness*" stemmed from the fact that, with five thousand acres surrounding his home, Monticello, he was a very happy man indeed.

We won't even go into what a slave owner like TJ might have meant by his "self-evident truth" that "all men are created equal." And as to the question of what our self-evident Creator had in mind when he created us, we wouldn't touch that one with a fluttering pixie.

INDUCTIVE LEAP
(DRAWING CONCLUSIONS FROM AMBIGUOUS EVIDENCE)

In the first century BCE, the political theorist and orator Cicero (106–43 BCE) declared, "To be ignorant of what happened before you were born is to remain always a child."

A couple of millennia later history repeated itself when Harvard philosopher George Santayana (1863–1952 CE) gave Cicero's warning this snappy tweaking: "Those who cannot remember the past are condemned to repeat it."

Political jabber hasn't been the same since.

Santayana's words have been appropriated by enough politicos and pundits to make a Google algorithm break into a sweat. These earnest counselors beseech us not to repeat history by, say, *going to war*, or *raising taxes*, or *legalizing whiskey*. They cite chapter and verse of historical precedents that give force to their warnings. "Don't go there again!" they exhort us. "Haven't you learned anything from past mistakes?"

But then, strangely, along come other earnest counselors who beseech us not to repeat history by *failing* to invade a particular country, or *lowering* taxes, or by making alcohol consumption *illegal*.

Santayana, we've got a problem. Two, actually.

The first is that the study of history is not as neat as, say, the study of rocks. History has way more variables than rocks do, so the enterprise of finding in it an exact replica of a current sociopolitical situation is virtually impossible. Consider the truism that history does not repeat itself; this makes the entire business of looking to past events for clues on how to make present choices dicey at best. Heraclitus clearly had this in mind when he said, "You don't step into the same river twice." All kinds of stuff keeps changing from one moment (and era) to the next, whether we like it or not—and not just the water.

So it is that, like the devil quoting the Bible, politicians and pundits can quote passages of history to draw opposing analogies to the same situation. Is the history we do not want to repeat in Iraq the appeasement of Germany or the quagmire of the Vietnam War? Judging by the outcomes of following their "historical lessons," the men and women who consider themselves students of history seem to pick the wrong analogy at a rate that is arguably worse than chance.

Add to this the fact that, historically speaking, historians are not always dependable, so the very foundation of historical lessons is shaky. Historians have been known to use dodgy

evidence, assailable sources, and even—heaven forbid—to give history a political spin.

But there is another, subtler problem with Santayana's historical pronouncement. It is not fallacious in itself, but there is an implicit conclusion that makes it fallacious. We are led to draw the conclusion that those who *do* remember the past are *not* condemned to repeat it. It just may be that those who study history and those who do not study history are *both* condemned to repeat it. In other words, everybody's doing it (repeating history), so you could make just as good a case that the study of history condemns people to repeat it.

"Lessons" of the Vietnam War

The pundits and pols all talk about the lessons of Vietnam. Unfortunately, they each seem to have a different lesson in mind. Here are the nominees for Best Lesson Bearer:

1. Melvin Laird, secretary of defense under President Richard Nixon, for: "Do not betray the people who are depending on you."
2. Major H. R. McMaster, author of *Dereliction of Duty*, for: "Military leaders should not be complicit in accepting the president's approach to war."
3. Former ambassador Francis Terry McNamara, author of *Escape with Honor*, for: "Don't cut and run."

4. Former chairman of the Joint Chiefs of Staff and former secretary of state General Colin Powell, for the Powell Doctrine: "Military action should be used only as a last resort and only if there is a clear risk to national security; if force must be used, it should be overwhelming and disproportionate to the force used by the enemy; there must be strong public support for the war; and there must be a clear exit strategy."

5. President George W. Bush, for: "One lesson [of Vietnam] is that we tend to want there to be instant success in the world, and the task in Iraq is going to take a while. . . . We'll succeed unless we quit."

6. Keith Olbermann, *Countdown*, MSNBC, for: "If you try to pursue a war for which the nation has lost its stomach, you and it are finished."

And the prize goes to: none of the above! The winner is the administration of President George W. Bush, for (and we're paraphrasing here): If you want to minimize public opposition to war, don't institute a draft.

ANALYTIC-SYNTHETIC SHUFFLE

One of the great logicians of our time—we speak, of course, of President George W. Bush—has apparently read Kant's *Critique of Pure Reason* (who are we to doubt his impressive reading list?). In any event, he does seem to have mastered what we call the old analytic-synthetic shuffle:

If the Iraqi regime is able to produce, buy, or steal an amount of highly enriched uranium a little larger than a single softball, it could have a nuclear weapon in less than a year.

— President GEORGE W. BUSH, October 7, 2002

Right, George. And if wishes were horses, then beggars would ride. But, as it turns out, wishes are not horses.

In an article in the October 8, 2002, edition of the online newsletter *CounterPunch*, Robert Jensen argues that the president's inflammatory statement is utterly meaningless. Jensen says it's equivalent to saying that if Iraq had a nuclear weapon, it would have a nuclear weapon, because the only difficult and time-consuming part of creating a nuclear weapon is getting your hands on the fissile material.

In other words, Jensen is claiming that the president is disguising an *analytic statement* as a *synthetic statement*. (That's philosophical shoptalk.)

To explain: *Analytic statements* are true by definition. "All U.S. senators are members of the legislative branch of government," is an *analytic statement*. It doesn't provide any new information about senators that we didn't already have. Could a sitting senator come along who wasn't a member of the legislative branch? No way: Senators are *by definition* members of the legislative branch. However, "All senators in 1924 were white males," is a *synthetic statement*. It tells us a novel fact about the composition of the Senate in that particular year, a fact that conceivably might have been otherwise—and actually has been otherwise for several decades.

How does this play out in Jensen's analysis of the president's statement? Jensen is arguing that the president's claim comes down to this: "Iraq could possibly make a nuclear bomb quickly if it had all the stuff it takes to make a nuclear bomb quickly." True by definition.

It's like the old vaudeville gag:

SHE: That third baseman is a terrific player.
HE: Hell, if I had his skills, I'd be that good too.

So why would President Bush try to pitch an uninformative statement like that to us? Could it be that in his zeal to make his case for invading Iraq, he was rhetorically stacking the deck? His statement *sounds* like it's informative, and it's definitely super scary, so much so that it sure could make a person favor a preemptive strike.

But the president doesn't stop there. He stacks the deck even more by emphasizing the *amount* of highly enriched uranium needed: hardly more than *a single softball's* worth!

Now maybe it really is easier to acquire a softball-size hunk of highly enriched uranium than it is to acquire a refrigerator-size hunk; maybe not. The president doesn't give us that information—not that he necessarily has it. And in either case, how easy is it? In our experience, getting our hands on the Hope Diamond, which is even *smaller* than a softball, has proven incredibly difficult. The point isn't that Bush is necessarily lying about the ultrascariness of a demented leader's needing only a small amount of fissile material to build a bomb. Nor is he necessarily wrong. It's rather that he's bullshitting.

PART IV

The *Star Trek* Strategy

Misleading by Creating an Alternate Universe

Nothing demonstrates the courage of politicos and pundits so stunningly as the way they handle themselves when caught in outright contradictions. Yes, sometimes they admit that "mistakes were made," a weasely phrase that ignores the question of who, exactly, made the mistakes. And occasionally they offer, "I misspoke," which suggests some kind of neurological slip-up that could happen to any innocent victim of a misfired synapse. But the truly brave and steadfast do not resort to such lame excuses. No, they appeal to a higher authority, the definition of truth itself. And by their revised definitions, they neither made mistakes nor misspoke; rather, they told the absolute truth—as defined in a galaxy far, far away.

REDEFINING TRUTH

Consider this epistemological parry by the master of make-believe, former president Ronald Reagan:

> *We did not—repeat, did not—trade weapons or anything else for hostages, nor will we.*
> — President RONALD REAGAN, November 13, 1986

> *Let me just say that it was not my intent to do business with Khomeini, to trade weapons for hostages.*
> — President RONALD REAGAN, December 6, 1986

> *A few months ago, I told the American people I did not trade arms for hostages. My heart and my best intentions still tell me that's true, but the facts and the evidence tell me it is not.*
> — President RONALD REAGAN, March 4, 1987, after reporters had stayed on the case and kept demonstrating that he had, in fact, traded arms for hostages

President Reagan's excuse for not coming clean on the arms-for-hostages exchange sets off cognitive dissonance alarms in the most softheaded of us. The Great Communicator sounds like a schoolboy who tells the teacher he didn't *really* dip Mary's pigtails in the inkwell, he only just kinda did it, in spite of himself. The schoolboy, like the GC, is hoping that his nondistinction will get by on a wink and a smile—an *argumentum ad misericordiam*, or the "appeal to sympathy," as in, "Hey, give me a break, will ya? I didn't really mean to do it. You know?"

"Americans should not become obsessed with the Iran arms scandal!"

But could it be that we are selling Reagan short? That he actually meant something he truly believed when he set up the opposition between what his heart and best intensions *still* told him was true and what the facts and evidence *also* told him was true, even if the latter contradicted the former? And if he did mean something, could he have been offering no less than alternative—and possibly coequal—ways of judging what is true?

Consider the paleontologist Marcus Ross, who wrote in his Ph.D. dissertation that mosasaurs, a species of marine reptile, vanished at the end of the Cretaceous era, about 65 million years ago. Dr. Ross also happens to be what is called a "young earth creationist" who believes the Bible is a literal account of the creation of the universe, and that the earth is at most ten thousand years old. Asked how he reconciles these views, Ross says that methods and theories of paleontology are one "paradigm" for studying the past, the scripture another. In other words, Ross is performing a trick that most philosophers have deemed impossible: holding two contradictory ideas in his mind at the same time. He has two different "paradigms" for determining the truth, and what is true under one paradigm is not necessarily true under the other. It is a kind of relativism we don't often associate with fundamentalists.

So perhaps President Reagan was saying something similar to what Dr. Ross said: His heart and intentions are one paradigm, the facts and evidence are another. But if you small-minded reporters are limiting the issue to facts and evidence, well, yeah, you're right.

* *

STACKING THE TRUTH TABLES

English-language philosophers have often accused their French counterparts of softheadedness and imprecision. To a British logical positivist like A. J. Ayer, for example, Jean-Paul Sartre wasn't worthy of being called a true philosopher because he spent his professional life thinking about unknowable subjects like the nature of being and existence and nothingness. For former French president Jacques Chirac, it is probably a relief that Ayer is no longer being; Ayer would have made mincemeat of Chirac's fanciful new theory of truth:

I would say that what is dangerous about this situation [in Iran] is not the fact of having a nuclear bomb—having one, maybe a second one a little later, well, that's not very dangerous.
— French president JACQUES CHIRAC, on a Monday

France, along with the international community, cannot accept the prospect of a nuclear-armed Iran.
— Statement from CHIRAC'S OFFICE, only hours later, which went on to denounce *the publication* of Chirac's previous comment as a "shameful campaign" and accuse the American media of "using any excuse to engage in France-bashing"

I should rather have paid attention to what I was saying and understood that perhaps I was on the record.
— French president JACQUES CHIRAC, on the following Tuesday

Just when we thought we'd never see a new theory of truth, along comes Jacques with a beaut. But before we go

FRENCH FRIED

there, let's review his predecessors in the annals of Western philosophy. There's the correspondence theory of truth, put forth by twentieth-century British philosophers Bertrand Russell and G. E. Moore: A belief is true if and only if there exists a fact corresponding to it. For example, "The cat is on the mat" is true if and only if there is, in fact, a cat on the mat.

Then there's the coherence theory of truth, subscribed to by the twentieth-century American philosopher Hilary Putnam: A belief is true if and only if it is part of an entire system of beliefs that is "consistent and harmonious." This one's harder to get one's mind around. According to this theory, "The cat is on the mat" is true if and only if it "fits" with the entire set of all beliefs held to be true. It must square, for example, with the belief that "material objects exist in spatio-temporal relation to each other"—but *also with* the belief that Joe DiMaggio was the American League MVP in 1941. *Whaaa?* The latter example sounds ridiculous only because "The cat is on the mat" obviously *is* compatible with the belief about DiMaggio's status. Why wouldn't it be compatible with that? But the point is that if somehow it *weren't* compatible with it, as some beliefs aren't (e.g., the belief that Ted Williams was the 1941 MVP is *not* compatible with the belief that DiMaggio was), then one or the other of them would be untrue. You'll just have to trust us on this one.

And then there's the pragmatist theory of truth, associated with the late nineteenth-century American philosophers Charles Sanders Peirce and William James: A belief is true if and only if it provokes action that leads to a desirable result.

Under this theory, "The cat is on the mat" is true if and only if my acting on it does not trip me up in some way. If believing "The cat is on the mat" to be true causes me to make a prediction that ends in an unsatisfactory result (e.g., I reach out to pet the alleged cat and my hand suffers a third-degree burn), then I may have to revise my belief that it is a cat that is on the mat.

Against this background comes President Chirac with a truth test that is truly unique. Yes, from the land that gave us Descartes and Pascal, we now get the public-record theory of truth, namely that a statement made to the media is true if and only if it is made "on the record." Under this theory, "The cat is on the mat" would be true if and only if it was consistent with official French foreign policy.

M. Chirac explains that what was wrong with his original, sunny take on Iran's acquiring nuclear weapons is that it wasn't intended for public consumption. France's official policy is that a nuclear Iran is unacceptable; therefore, the media should not have reported his statement contradicting that position. *Vive la vérité!*

(Full disclosure: Our own hidden assumption is that anything true is reportable, a position not shared by many governments, some closer than France.)

WHITE LIES

An alternate universe we are all familiar with is the universe of white lies, statements that aren't strictly true, but then again

aren't quite whoppers either. They exist in a sort of neth-
erworld. "How are you this morning?" "Fine, thank you."
Translation: "Actually, my corns hurt, but I don't want to go
there, and I am *basically* fine. Well, sort of fine."

President Reagan's aide Michael Deaver told the following
white lie when he was asked how the president had reacted
to Congress's authorization of the sale of planes to Saudi
Arabia: "[The president said], 'Thank God!'"

Actually, what the president said was, *"I feel like I've just
crapped a pineapple!"* [iv]

The comment did have a certain down-home spontaneity
going for it, but Mr. Deaver judged that it sounded unpresi-
dential, so substituted the less memorable, but more spiritual
"Thank God!"

Although we're generally sticklers when it comes to truth
telling, we believe Deaver made a good call on this one. God
knows we've heard worse white lies, like when Bill Clinton
said with utmost sincerity, "Since I was a little boy, I've heard
about the Iowa caucuses. That's why I would really like to
do well in them." History tells us otherwise: Iowa began
having caucuses when Clinton was in graduate school, and
precocious as Bill was, he was out of short pants by grad
school.

Or when Al Gore said that his mother used to lull him
to sleep as a baby by singing "Look for the Union Label," a
jingle written when Al was twenty-seven. Here, Al opened
himself up to the accusation that his mother was still singing
him lullabies beyond an appropriate age.

"It wasn't a lie, Senator, it was a larger truth."

The dangers of the white lie are illustrated by the story of Alice Grayson:

Alice was supposed to bake a cake for the Baptist Church Ladies' Group bake sale but forgot to do it until the last minute. This cake was important to Alice because she wanted so badly to make a good impression. So, being inventive, she looked around the house for a way to fashion a quick substitute.

Alice found it in the bathroom—a roll of toilet paper. She plunked it into a dish and covered it with icing. The finished product looked beautiful.

Before she left the house to drop the cake off at the church and head for work, Alice woke her daughter, gave her some money, and instructed her to be at the bake sale the moment it opened, at 9:30 A.M., to buy the cake and bring it home. But when Alice's daughter arrived at the sale, she found the beautiful cake had already been sold. When Alice heard the news, she was horrified—everyone would know!

The next day, Alice promised herself she would try not to think about the cake; she would attend the fancy luncheon at the home of a fellow church member and try to have a good time. The meal was elegant, the company was definitely upper-crust, but to Alice's horror, the cake in question was presented for dessert! Alice felt the blood drain from her face. She started out of her chair to confess, but before she could get to her feet, the mayor's wife exclaimed, "What a beautiful cake!"

To which Alice heard the proud hostess reply, "Thank you, I baked it myself."

BUYING CONVENTIONAL WISDOM

That old philosopher, Anonymous, once wisely said, "To choose a word is to choose a world," meaning that the terms used to define an issue limit the ways we are able to think about it. By buying into the conventional wisdom thrown at us constantly by politicians and the media, we help the pols and pundits create an alternate universe of discourse that determines what can and can't be said on a given subject:

(Montage on *The Daily Show* with Jon Stewart)

He [Kerry] stands way out of the mainstream.
— FOX NEWS

[Kerry's] way out of the mainstream.
— Spokesman for Bush camp

He stands so far out of the mainstream.
— Communication director, Bush-Cheney campaign

He's so out of the mainstream.
— LYNNE CHENEY

[Kerry and Edwards are] . . . well out of the mainstream.
— GOP strategist

I'm getting a feeling. I think, I think [Kerry and Edwards are] out of the mainstream.
— JON STEWART

How does conventional wisdom become conventional? As Stewart informs us, it usually starts with talking points. Party A decides how it wants us to think about the candidates of party B and then sets out to get their unflattering labels repeated so often in the media that they stick in our minds. The media cooperate because it gives them a hook for their stories. And we, the public, are only too glad to latch onto these labels, because they're so catchy. And more significantly, it's way easier than thinking.

As the essayist Louis Menand points out in a *New Yorker* piece entitled "Notable Quotables," when it comes to popular quotes, catchiness trumps accuracy. Sherlock Holmes never said, "Elementary, my dear Watson." Nor did Ilsa, Ingrid Bergman's character in *Casablanca*, ever say, "Play it again, Sam." Horace Greeley never said, "Go west, young man," and Patrick Henry never uttered the words "Give me liberty, or give me death." And most disappointingly, Leo Durocher never said, "Nice guys finish last." What Durocher *did* say was, "The nice guys are all over there, in seventh place," which clearly lacks the sine qua non of a memorable quote: catchiness! The true Durocher line doesn't sing;

it has no poetry; and it's far too long. As the political operatives say, "Give me catchy, or give me dirt!"

So we, the unwashed, unwittingly end up as coconspirators in the media's wordplay game. When Bush comes up in conversation, we automatically pronounce him "incurious." Like voice-activated robots, we repeat that Obama "isn't experienced enough," that Cheney is "Darth Vader" and is "the real president," that Hillary is "bitchy," that Bill was "slick" and "undisciplined." Never mind that these labels all have a grain of truth in them. They wouldn't work if they didn't resonate with us in some way. The problem is that they become a substitute for thought. Surely Calvin Coolidge was something besides silent and Nixon something besides tricky. Well, scratch that last one.

ACQUIRING CONVENTIONAL WISDOM THE OLD-FASHIONED WAY

We turn again to our friends at the mythical Armenian Radio:

RADIO LISTENER: What is an exchange of ideas?

GOVERNMENT OFFICIAL: That is when you go into the commissar's office with your own idea and come out with his.

CONVENTIONAL FOLLY

Writing in the *Los Angeles Times*, Michael May asks how it can be that government experts nearly always fail to see the big event coming: the disintegration of the Soviet Union, the rise of China as a capitalist power. His answer: the bounds of conventional wisdom. The right questions don't get asked because they are not on the list of questions du jour. While officials are trying to figure out whether the Soviets will develop a first-strike nuclear capability, the Soviet Union comes unraveled. If some poor forecaster had predicted the Soviet breakup, May thinks, that analyst would have been immediately marginalized.

If you need further proof of how conventional assumptions can keep us from thinking outside the box, consider the following story:

Jesus was making his usual rounds in heaven when he noticed a wizened, white-haired old man sitting in a corner looking very disconsolate.

"See here, old fellow," said Jesus kindly, "this is heaven. The sun is shining, you've got all you could want to eat, all the instruments you might want to play—you're supposed to be blissfully happy! What's wrong?"

"Well," said the old man, "you see, I was a carpenter on earth, and lost my dearly beloved son at an early age. And here in heaven I was hoping more than anything to find him."

Tears sprang to Jesus's eyes. "FATHER!" he cried.

The old man jumped to his feet, bursting into tears, and shouted, "PINOCCHIO!"

The joke works because we, the readers, fall into the gag writer's trap of making the conventional assumption.

EMPTY PRINCIPLES

Another alternate universe that can come in handy is the Universe of Vacuous Ethical Principles—lofty principles that are so abstract they encompass just about anything, or possibly, nothing. This must have been W's intent when he lofted this one our way, as he vetoed legislation permitting federally funded embryonic stem cell research:

Destroying human life in the hopes of saving human life is not ethical.

The Ethicist-in-Chief's final word on the subject caught our eye right off the bat because we've always had a soft spot in our hearts for the Ethical. In fact, it's right up there with the Red Sox and the Folies Bergère as one of our favorite things.

But unfortunately we went to school way before children were left behind, and that takes all the fun out of this pronouncement made by the Ethicker (as he calls himself). We're thinking particularly of our reading of that eighteenth-century German pronouncement pooper Immanuel Kant.

Manny maintained that rational ethical actions must stem from principles or maxims "whose universality as a law you can at the same time will," and further, that this is the "only condition under which a will can never come into conflict with itself." Now we admit that our German is severely limited ("Salzkartoffel" and "Gerstensaft" pretty much exhaust our vocabulary), and that even in translation Kant is one abstruse *Kartoffel*. But at least one thing he is saying is that if you're going to justify one action by an absolute principle, your other actions need to be consistent with that same principle. Come to think of it, our Cub Scout leader taught us more or less the same thing.

So what are we to make of Principled George's penchant for executing human beings in unparalleled numbers during his term as governor of Texas? He's on record as saying capital punishment serves as a deterrent of possible future murders and rapes, which sounds an awful lot like he's following a principle that says "It's okay to take a human life in the hopes of saving another human life." And that just doesn't seem to gel with his pronouncement that "[d]estroying human life in the hopes of saving human life is not ethical." Actually, it sounds more like its opposite.

"I keep my core beliefs written on my palm for easy reference."

But, hey, maybe we're just quibbling. Going from an abstract principle to a particular ethical issue is always a dicey business, as any medical ethicist will tell you. Take the doctor in the following story:

A woman is in her doctor's office, when she suddenly shouts out, "Doctor, kiss me!"

The doctor looks at her and says that it would be against his code of ethics to kiss her.

About twenty minutes later the woman again shouts out, "Doctor, please, kiss me, just once!"

Again he refuses, apologetically, but says that as a doctor he simply cannot kiss her.

Another twenty minutes pass, and the woman pleads with the doctor, "Doctor, Doctor, please kiss me, just once!!"

"Look," he says, "I am sorry. I just *cannot* kiss you. In fact, I probably shouldn't even be sleeping with you."

Come to think of it, maybe we've totally misjudged Mr. Bush. Perhaps he isn't a Kantian after all, but a Marxist—as in Groucho, whose aperçu on ethics we never tire of quoting: "Those are my principles; if you don't like them, I have others."

—ᴍ—

Extra Credit

Misleading with Way Twisty Formal Fallacies

When our mothers admonished us to mind our p's and q's, we may have taken them too literally and ended up in that modern philosopher's paradise, the Realm of Formal Logic, a place where p's and q's need some serious minding. Suffice it to say, it ain't paradise for everybody.

Yet for those brave souls who never met a p or q they didn't like, we offer this Extra Credit Chapter on Formal Fallacies, mistakes in deductive logic. To be sure, this kind of faulty reasoning leads to some of the most reprehensible conclusions politicos throw our way, but to detect these errors, we need to do some brain-throbbing cogitatin'.

(If it helps to read this section out loud, we suggest a padded room, far from family and intimate friends.)

IMPROPER TRANSPOSITION—OR MAYBE NOT

Playing fast and loose with logic offers politicos and their retinues so many options for deceit, keeping track of them can be difficult. That is why they always carry their fast-and-loose-with-logic playbook. In it, you'll find the slipperiest play of them all, the double reverse:

> TAVIS SMILEY (INTERVIEWER): *How are you going to respond to folks on the campaign trail when they ask what qualifies you to be the commander-in-chief, given that you have not served in the country's military?*

> AL SHARPTON (INTERVIEWEE): *I think that just because one served in the military does not make one a competent commander-in-chief.*

The interpretations of this exchange have more levels than a La-Z-Boy recliner, so we're going to assign them numbers:

   1. At first blush, it seems clear that Reverend Sharpton is responding to a different question than the one Mr. Smiley asked. We know that Sharpton is sharp, so we seriously doubt he is *unwittingly* answering a different question than the one Smiley posed. But then why does he do it?

   2. A good guess (and one that some pundits subscribed to in their blogs) is that Reverend Sharpton was actually taking a bold stand against the fallacy of improper transposition, a fundamental no-no for any student of Aristotle. This fallacy

* *

points to the bad logic of alleging the following: If p, then q. Therefore, if not p, then not q. That would be like saying, "If Osama's alive, he's in Tora Bora, so if he's dead, he must be somewhere else." It just doesn't follow, and Reverend Sharpton would be properly instructing Mr. Smiley in the folly of this common fallacy.

3. But hold the phone! For Sharpton to be catching Smiley in this clumsy error of reasoning, Sharpton would have to maintain that what Smiley basically said was, "If one did not serve in the military, then one is not qualified to be commander-in-chief" (which Smiley pretty much did suggest), *and, therefore,* "if one did serve in the military, one is qualified to be commander-in-chief" (which Smiley definitely *did not* say or suggest).

4. So what's going on here? Since Smiley definitely did not say that if one did serve in the military, one *is* qualified to be commander-in-chief, what is Sharpton getting at? Could it be that he wanted us to think that the other candidates—like John Kerry—who *did* serve in the military could be just as incompetent as he is to be commander-in-chief, so we might as well vote for Sharpton?

That would sure make for a ringing campaign slogan: "Vote for me—I'm probably no more incompetent than anybody else!"

He's got our vote.

5. But perhaps the reverend is simply implying (albeit in a convoluted way) that it's some other quality *that he himself possesses,* and not simply service in the military, that makes for a competent commander-in-chief.

TUCKING FALSE PREMISE INTO VALID ARGUMENT

One of the cleverest of the bull-slinger's tactics is to sneak a false premise into a dazzlingly valid argument. This may be the origin of the expression "Dazzle them with bullshit."

> *If [the glove] doesn't fit, you must acquit!*
> — The late defense attorney JOHNNIE COCHRAN, in his
>   summation to the jury in the O. J. Simpson murder trial

Cochran's couplet is as snappy and memorable as the best TV ad slogans. But logical? Not so much.

First some background: The glove in question was found near the murder scene and became part of the prosecution's list of items of circumstantial evidence linking Simpson to the murder; the prosecution produced expert witnesses avowing that the glove, *in better condition,* would fit Simpson. The glove's condition at the time of the trial had been compromised by being soaked in blood, mutilated in the crime laboratory, and repeatedly frozen and unfrozen, so the prosecution resisted having the defendant actually try it on. But goaded on by Cochran, the prosecution finally relented, Simpson tried the glove on (over latex gloves, to avoid forensic contamination), and it apparently did *not* fit—at least in its present condition and in the present circumstances.

That did it! Cochran's rhetorical genius was not only in the catchiness of his line, but in its metaphorical implications: If the circumstantial evidence *altogether* does not fit (does not meet a reasonable standard of believability), then you must acquit (on the basis of reasonable doubt).

But what Cochran actually did was to tuck a faulty premise into a valid denying-the-consequent wrapper. Like all valid forms of argument, denying the consequent will lead inexorably to a true conclusion—*unless* it starts from a false premise. How so? Denying the consequent takes the following form: If *p*, then *q*. Not *q;* therefore, not *p*. Or, "If Muffy is a cat, then Muffy is an animal. Muffy is *not* an animal; therefore, Muffy is *not* a cat." Valid as a brand-new driver's license, right?

So Cochran argued as follows:

A. If Simpson is the murderer, then the glove found at the crime scene will fit him.
B. The glove found at the crime scene does not fit him.
C. Therefore, Simpson is not the murderer.

The argument is *valid*, but that does not necessarily mean that it leads to a *true conclusion*. Valid forms of argument are like computers: garbage in, garbage out. The trick lies in A: It is a false premise. The glove could belong to, say, Mrs. McGillicutty down the street, who happened to be walking her dog in the area prior to the murder, or it could belong to Simpson but not fit him anymore, for any one of a variety of reasons. So the assumption of A is unjustified, and Simpson could still be the murderer without fitting neatly into the glove.

There's a joke that perfectly illustrates the phenomenon of a valid argument leading to a false conclusion:

Kevin thought he was dead, when in reality he was very much alive. His delusion became such a problem that his family finally paid for him to see a psychiatrist.

The psychiatrist spent many laborious sessions trying to convince Kevin that he was still alive. Nothing seemed to work. Finally the doctor tried one last approach. He took out his medical books and proceeded to show the patient that dead men don't bleed. After hours of tedious study, Kevin seemed convinced that dead men, in fact, don't bleed.

"Do you now agree that dead men don't bleed?" the doctor asked.

"Yes, I do," replied Kevin.

"Very well, then," the doctor said. He took out a pin and pricked Kevin's finger. Out came a trickle of blood. The doctor asked, "What does that tell you?"

"Oh, my goodness!" Kevin exclaimed, as he stared incredulously at his finger. "Dead men *do* bleed!!"

The psychiatrist has argued:

If you're dead, then you don't bleed (if p, then q).
You did bleed (not q).
Therefore, you're not dead (not p).

The psychiatrist is denying the consequent when he says, "You did bleed" and concludes that Kevin isn't dead. That's a valid argument, and he expects Kevin to therefore accept the conclusion.

Kevin does in fact accept the validity of the argument, but because he's convinced the conclusion is false, he reasons that the major premise must be false. Garbage in, garbage out.

And that's what's so fetching about a denying the consequent argument. If A and B *were* true, C would be true as well, so we can get caught up in the validity of the argument while the false premise glides right past us. Which is why we always say, "If the premise doesn't fit, it don't mean s—t."

DENYING THE ANTECEDENT—NOT!

If you think that was tricky, check out the logical debate behind the arguments over gun control:

A well regulated militia, being necessary to the security of a free state, the right of the people to keep and bear arms, shall not be infringed.
— SECOND AMENDMENT, U.S. Constitution

In the twentieth century, the Second Amendment has become an anachronism, largely because of drastic changes in the militia it was designed to protect. We no

*longer have the citizen militia like that of the eighteenth
century. Today's equivalent of a "well-regulated"
militia—the National Guard—has more limited
membership than its early counterpart and depends on
government-supplied, not privately owned, firearms.
Gun control laws have no effect on the arming of today's
militia. . . . Therefore, they raise no serious Second
Amendment issues.*

— Position paper of the BRADY CAMPAIGN to Prevent Gun
    Violence: "The Second Amendment: Myth and Meaning"

*If, for argument's sake, a civilian "well-regulated
militia" is no longer "necessary to the preservation of a
free [s]tate," it does not logically follow that "the right of
the people to keep and bear arms" may now be infringed.
To so conclude would be to commit the fallacy of denying
the antecedent.*

— STEPHEN HALBROOK, constitutional lawyer

Did we hear that right? The policy wonks at the Brady
Campaign made a silly logical mistake in their argument?
Does this mean that all the Supreme Court needs to do is to
spot that egregious error in reasoning and—*poof!*—end of
discussion of the whole right-to-bear-arms controversy?

Say it isn't so!

Okay, it isn't so. But the anti-gun-control advocates sure
had us going there for a while.

* *

Let us review.

The fallacy of denying the antecedent goes like this: If *p*, then *q*. Not *p;* therefore, not *q*. Or, in feline terms, "If Muffy is a cat, then Muffy is an animal. Muffy is *not* a cat; therefore, Muffy is *not* an animal." *Way fallacious!* Just ask Dan's dog, Muffy.

Now, let's take a nonfeline gander at the Brady bunch's proposition. They seem to be arguing that the Second Amendment is logically equivalent to saying, "*If* a well-regulated militia (with privately owned guns) is necessary to the security of a free state, *then* the right of the people to keep and bear arms shall not be infringed." Then they suggest that a well-regulated militia (with privately owned guns) is no longer necessary to the security of a free state, and, therefore, the right of the people to keep and bear arms *can be* infringed.

To which the pro-gun people respond: Aha! *That's* the formal fallacy of denying the antecedent. The framers of the Constitution could still have logically thought that the right to bear arms is uninfringeable, *regardless* of whether a well-regulated militia is necessary to the security of a free state, just as Muffy could still be an animal, even though she's not a cat.

It's at that point that, heads spinning, we head for cover. But as fate would have it, while hiding behind a stone wall, we're buttonholed by a wizened wise man with the following point:

*"I wonder if future generations will realize that
their forefathers were such gun nuts?"*

"Don't you see? The problem with both arguments is that the Constitution was not written by logicians, but by ordinary mortals. To figure out what they meant, we have to ask questions that are more *psychological* than *logical*. Questions like, Why would the framers have even bothered to mention the need for a well-regulated militia if they thought it made no difference to the inviolability of the right to keep and bear arms? In other words, the framers may have meant to say, 'If *and only if* a well-regulated militia is necessary to the security of a free state, the right to keep and bear arms may not be infringed.' And if that's what they meant, then the fallacy of denying the antecedent has *not* occurred. After all, it's perfectly valid to say, 'if **and only if** p, then q; not p; therefore, not q.'

"But on the other hand, would the founders have been likely to use one of their favorite terms, 'right,' in conjunction with the idea of a *permissible* infringement? You could say that in the minds of the framers, rights in general were considered uninfringeable, so maybe the bit about the necessity of a well-regulated militia isn't all that germane to the argument after all.[v]

"In other words, if questions of constitutional interpretation could be settled by formal logic, we wouldn't call it interpretation."

And then the wizened wise man disappeared into the woods, leaving us without a logical fallacy to gripe about. But then again, he also left us without a solution to the Second Amendment controversy.

AFFIRMING THE CONSEQUENT

On the list of mind-boggling illogical formulations, the formal fallacy known as affirming the consequent is right up there with denying the antecedent.

> *[W]hat's fun about covering politics these days is that half the hysterics think we're liberal apologists, and the other half think we're conservative shills.* **If they're both mad at you, you know you're doing your job.**
> — *Washington Post* chief political reporter SHAILAGH MURRAY, on Washington Post Radio

This one is super tricky. You may want to take notes. It's the fallacy of turning a valid proposition around and claiming that the new version must also be true. Using symbols, it's expressed like this: If p, then q; q, therefore p. And using an example, it's like saying, "You're only at the office on weekdays; it's a weekday, so you must be at the office."

Not so fast, buddy! It's your vacation!

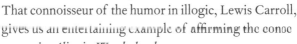

That connoisseur of the humor in illogic, Lewis Carroll, gives us an entertaining example of affirming the consequent, in *Alice in Wonderland*:

PIGEON: [to Alice] *You're a serpent; and there's no use denying it. I suppose you'll be telling me next that you never tasted an egg!*

* *

> ALICE: *I have tasted eggs, certainly, but little girls eat eggs quite as much as serpents do, you know.*
>
> PIGEON: *If they do, why, then they're a kind of serpent.*

And now back to Ms. Murray in the studio. Let's grant that if you're doing your job as a reporter, both left-wingers and right-wingers will be at your throat. But it doesn't follow that if left-wingers and right-wingers are both at your throat, you are necessarily doing your job. Both sides might be infuriated by a reporter because she's so damned defensive or has a really bad haircut.

AT LAST, A CORRECT SYLLOGISM

And finally, here's a sweet little change of pace—a politician who actually employs strict, Aristotelian logic *correctly*. The official in the exchange below is invoking a basic QED (Roman text messaging for *quod erat demonstrandum*, literally "which was to be demonstrated"). In so doing, he gets his opponent to hoist himself by his own petard, always a pleasure for petard fans.

> (A delegate to the Utah Republican Convention was arguing that a fence should be constructed along the entire U.S.-Mexican border, to prevent illegal immigrants from entering.)
>
> GOP OFFICIAL: *What happens when they [illegals] climb the fence?*

DELEGATE: *You electrify it. Then they won't touch it.*

OFFICIAL: *But what if they touch it? You would let them die?*

DELEGATE: *It would be their choice.*

OFFICIAL: *What about a mother with a baby strapped to her back? You would let the mother and the baby die?*

DELEGATE: *It would be the mother's choice to kill that baby.*

OFFICIAL: *Then you're in favor of abortion?*

[Dead silence]

— As reported by PAUL ROLLY in the *Salt Lake Tribune*

Nicely done, GOP official!

Your model, clearly, is the deductive argument known as the syllogism, as in, "All men are mortal. Socrates is a man; therefore, Socrates is mortal." In this case, "All people who willfully play a role in the killing of a child are in principle the same as pro-abortionists. The delegate is willing to play a role in the killing of a child; therefore, the delegate is the same as a pro-abortionist." (The fact that the first premise is debatable doesn't matter here, as both official and delegate apparently accept it.)

But what is particularly refreshing in this scenario is the clueless delegate who suffers a self-inflicted wound in what is known as *pugio tuus est interfector tuus*—literally "your own dagger is your killer." There are *pugio tuus* gags in virtually every culture, but our favorite is this golden oldie:

A beggar was going door-to-door asking for alms, because his house was destroyed in a fire.

"Do you have a document from the police confirming that your story is true?" a housewife asked him.

"Alas"—the beggar sighed—"that was destroyed in the fire too."

In *Hamlet*, Shakespeare contributed the English equivalent of *pugio tuus est interfector tuus* with the lines "For 'tis the sport to have the engineer / Hoist with his own petard," which means it's fun to cause the bomb maker to be blown up with his own bomb—the word *petard* referring to a medieval bomb used to breach fortifications. (We refuse to find any significance in the fact that *petard* comes from a Middle French word meaning the "expulsion of intestinal gas.")

And speaking of gas, let's get back to Aristotle and his Washington traveling companion, the aardvark. After walking around town taking in the usual power centers— the White House, the Hill, K Street—the aardvark turned to Aristotle and said, "You know what? You ought to run for president. You're way smarter than any of these people, you're an expert on logic and rhetoric, and you've got terrific name recognition."

"Not for me, pal," Aristotle replied. "I'm a behind-the-scenes kind of guy, the Karl Rove of the Golden Age."

"You're kidding me. Whose campaign did you run?" Aardy asked.

"Well, do you remember that putz they used to call Alexander the Mediocre?"

—ɯ—

The Debates

Misleading by Fabrication (Ours)

Democratic presidential candidates have been reaching out to "theme" audiences by participating in debates on cable television's "niche" channels. They've famously responded to questions and traded barbs on Logo (gay and lesbian), YouTube/CNN, and PBS. But less reported are the candidates' appearances on other special-interest channels. Herewith, some highlights from those programs.

Food Network

RACHAEL RAY: Hi, Hillary. Golly, you look nice. Do you cook in a pantsuit?

HILLARY CLINTON: That's a great question, Rachel. A truly wonderful question that resonates with me and all the other hard-working women and girls in this fabulous country of ours.

RAY: So, do you?

CLINTON: Well, of course I can't speak for Michelle Obama on this question—if she wants to cook in a pantsuit, I think that's her prerogative. That's what this country is all about, freedom to cook in whatever garb you choose.

RAY: Listen, we've only got three minutes before I have to take the soufflé out of the oven. Do you cook in a pantsuit, Senator?

CLINTON: Yes and no. I would cook in a pantsuit. As I've said many times, there is nothing wrong with cooking that way. But actually—and the record shows this to be true—I don't cook. Not that I think there is anything wrong with cooking, that is, if . . .

RAY: Wow! Would you look at this soufflé?

CLINTON: Fabulous! Can I have your recipe?

Home & Garden

KAHI LEE: Representative Dennis Kucinich, your apartment here in Cleveland is adorable! Where did you ever get the idea of oilcloth for your kitchen table?

DENNIS KUCINICH: To tell you the truth, Kahi, it's the only tablecloth I was able to find that wasn't manufactured in a sweatshop in a country that's a signatory to the NAFTA treaty. I made it myself from an old tarpaulin,

LEE: That is too creative! And your curtains! Made to look like old sails!

KUCINICH: Those *are* old sails, Kahi. China has taken all our curtain factories, displacing American curtain workers. Until we bring those jobs back to the U.S., I'm going to keep on looking for the label of the American Sailmakers Union.

LEE: I can't wait to see what you do with the West Wing after your inauguration!

KUCINICH: What are you smoking, Kahi?

E!

ROBERT VERDI (*FASHION POLICE* HOST): Johnny, Johnny, what a delicious little mess you are tonight. You're just screaming, "Help me! Help me! I haven't found my inner style!"

JOHN EDWARDS: There are two Americas, Robert. The "haves" and the "have-nots."

VERDI: Tell me about it, Johnny. You either have that fabulous look-me-over flair or you don't. And darling, what can I say? You look like a choirboy in a wind tunnel. First, we just have to do something with that hair. [*Sotto voce*] You're not wearing a rug, are you, pet?

EDWARDS: Before I say anything, Robert, I want to say that I'd rather lose this race than compromise the principles I hold close to my heart.

VERDI: Are you thinking the same thing I am? A pendant on a gold chain? Brilliant! But something tasteful, Johnny. I'm thinking an American flag in rubies and emeralds.

EDWARDS: I don't want to come off as ostentatious.

VERDI: Of course not, pet. But rhinestones are sooo tacky, don't you agree?

Animal Planet

KINKAJOU (OF *MEERKAT MANOR*): Governor Richardson, you've been accused of speciesism ever since your quip that you'd like to see Osama bin Laden dead as a dormouse. Do you regret your remark?

BILL RICHARDSON: Well, uh, it was, uh, just a way, you know, of speaking. I could have said, "dead as a mackerel" or "dead as a hippopotamus," for that matter. But that doesn't mean—

KINKAJOU: Let's get straight to the point, Governor. Do you see being a dormouse as a lifestyle choice?

RICHARDSON: It, uh, depends on what you mean by choice. Like, did I choose to be too big for my suit jacket? Or, more to the point, would I, personally, choose to be a dormouse?

MTV

MC: This one here's for my man La Bamba there. Yo, dawg, my posse sayin' you ain't got no street cred. So how you gonna keep it real with yo' homeboys, know what I'm sayin'?

BARACK OBAMA: Could you repeat the question?

MC: No, fool, that's the onliest shot you get. Same question for Hill.

HILLARY CLINTON: Yo, bro, I ain't no ho'. I'm good in the hood, but I never would (not that I should), but I sure as hell could. Two roads diverged in a yellow wood. And that, dawg, makes all the diff.

Those of you who have been reading this book merely for idle amusement may wish to stop here, kick up your feet, and grab a wine cooler. But for those of you who see life as a relentless series of tests, we wouldn't want to disappoint you.

Incidentally, this one only counts as 35% of your overall grade.

Match the fallacies to the examples in this made-up election speech. Extra credit for Latin nomenclature.

1. **Affirming the consequent**

2. **Appeal to authority, with a hint of "God is my charioteer"** *(Deus est auriga meus)*

3. **Bad company, or guilt by association**

4. **Contextomy**

5. *Cum hoc ergo propter hoc*

6. **False dilemma**

7. **Naturalistic fallacy**

8. **Slippery slope argument**

9. **Weak analogy**

10. **Weasel words**

My Fellow Americans,

(a) My opponent has told you she believes flame-throwers are not protected by the Second Amendment. That's right—she thinks the right to throw flames should be denied innocent American men, women, and children. Think about that for a moment. Who else in history thought Americans shouldn't have flamethrowers? You've got it—Adolf Hitler!

(b) But my opponent asks, "What use would a law-abiding American citizen have for a flamethrower anyway?" That's not the point! Today they'll regulate flamethrowers; tomorrow it will be assault rifles; pretty soon they'll be outlawing water pistols!

(c) My opponent points to the increase in flamethrower-related violence in the past ten years. First of all, what she calls "murder and mayhem" I call "friendly fire."

(d) Furthermore, what she doesn't tell you is that this increase was accompanied by increased cure rates for cancer, heart disease, and stroke.

(e) Flame is one of the last things in the world that ought to be regulated. Fire, after all, is one of the four basic elements—right up there with earth, wind, and water.

(f) There's an old saying, "If it ain't broke, don't fix it." Well, we haven't regulated flamethrowers heretofore, so it follows that the situation ain't broke, right?

(g) To outlaw flamethrowers because they can be used in robberies or arson would be like outlawing little kittens because they can be used as projectiles.

(h) Take it from no less an expert than the man who played Moses in *The Ten Commandments*, Charlton Heston, who said, "There's no such thing as a good flamethrower; there's no such thing as a bad flamethrower."

(i) Contrast those wise words with my opponent's defeatist position, in which—in an apparent reference to flamethrowers—she says, "Four score and seven . . . honored dead . . . shall . . . perish from the earth." As for me, I say that a nation armed with appropriate incendiary devices shall never perish!

(j) Therefore, my fellow Americans, make no mistake. The question of flamethrower control comes down to this: Are you for freedom or are you for totalitarianism?

Answers: a–3, b–8, c–10, d–5, e–7, f–1, g–9, h–2, i–4, j–6

Scoring: Multiply the number of correct answers by 10 and subtract 5 points for neatness.

Selected Bios of Bullshitters

—∿—

Boxer, Barbara Levy. Lefty, Jewish, feminist, Bay Area senator. For a pundit or political foe, each one of these characteristics would be enough to launch an explosive stereotype—but put all together, they are a regular Hindenburg.

Bush, Barbara. First mother, definitely not Jewish or from San Francisco.

Bush, George Walker. Former governor of Texas, and forty-third president of the United States, Bush is the son of George Herbert Walker Bush, forty-first president of the U.S.A. As noted earlier, when asked if he had consulted his father about invading Iraq, G. W. Bush replied that there is a higher father to whom he appealed. It is generally assumed that this higher father was Dick Cheney (see below).

Cheney, Richard "Dick" Bruce. Secretary of defense under Bush I, winner of the Presidential Medal of Freedom in 1991 for "preserving America's defenses at a time of great change around the world," two-term vice president under Bush II, husband of Lynne Cheney, an author of dirty books, and father of Mary, who just happens to be a lesbian, not that it's any of your business. Known variously as "Darth Vader," "Haliburton Hal," and "Mr. Death," Mr. Cheney is said to always have the president's ear, which he apparently keeps in an undisclosed location.

Chicks, Dixie. Sexist-monikered American singing group who publically expressed displeasure with their president; for a short period afterward their record sales dipped, but ultimately they made a comeback, unlike the president.

Chirac, Jacques René. Former president of France and mayor of Paris. Renowned for speaking political double-talk fluently in two languages, Jacques René dresses his freedom fries with *l'huile*.

Clinton, William "Bill" Jefferson. Former governor of Arkansas and forty-second president of the United States (1993–2001), Clinton is regarded as a political centrist, who occasionally assumed liberal postures, most frequently in the Oval Office. Mr. Clinton is the husband of 2008 Democratic presidential candidate Hillary Rodham Clinton, whom he owes big-time.

DeLay, Thomas "the Hammer" Dale. Former conservative Republican representative from Texas's Twenty-second Congressional District, although the numeric designation of that district is subject to change, pending redistricting. In 2005, Mr. DeLay was indicted by a grand jury on criminal charges involving campaign finance irregularities and subsequently withdrew his name from reelection. In May 2007, he led a Washington, D.C., "Campaigns and Elections" seminar devoted to ethics. (Honest to God, we don't make this stuff up.)

Falwell, Jerry Laymon, Sr. (deceased May 15, 2007). A fundamentalist Christian pastor and televangelist, Falwell was the founder of the Moral Majority, a lobby group for good values. After the 9/11 terrorist attacks, Falwell famously said, "I really believe that the pagans, and the abortionists, and the feminists, and the gays and the lesbians who are actively trying to make that an alternative lifestyle, the ACLU, People For the American Way, all of them who have tried to secularize America. I point the finger in their face and say 'you helped this happen.'" Interestingly, no pagan has ever denied the allegation.

Gore, Albert "Al" Arnold, Jr. Forty-fifth vice president of the U.S.A. (sandwiched between Quayle and Cheney) under Bill Clinton, Albert was the Democratic candidate for president in 2000; he lost that race by a whisker and a chad, to coin a phrase. Gore once stated that he invented the Internet, but his words were misconstrued. What he really said was that due to a sticky situation in the Oval Office, he invented the intern net.

Hitler, Adolf (1889–1945). Failed artist who went on to become a successful politician and mass murderer, thus enhancing the value of his canvases on eBay.

Jefferson, Thomas (1743–1836). Third president of the U.S.A., architect, wordsmith (principal author of the D of I), inventor, horticulturist, slave owner, and adulterer. He is one of our Founding Fathers, also one of our Foundling Fathers.

Kerry, John. Ceremoniously decorated and subsequently unceremoniously auto-undecorated, Vietnam War veteran, junior senator from Massachusetts, and Democratic candidate for president (2004; some say he lost). Dubbed by his opponents a "flip-flopper" because he uttered such statements as "I actually did vote for the $87 billion before I voted against it." What's the fuss?

Khan, Genghis (1162–1227). Politician and military leader who founded the Mongol Empire, one of the largest in history. Although much of the world still regards him as a ruthless and bloodthirsty conqueror, present-day Mongols still refer to him as "The Khan" or "The Dude."

McCarthy, Joseph Raymond (1908–1957). Republican senator from Wisconsin (1947–1957) known for his crusade against

Communism in the House Un-American Activities Committee. Those hearings were televised and popularized McCarthy's day-old-shave look, taken up by Richard Nixon (see below) and still seen today on *American Idol.*

Nixon, Richard Milhous (1913–1994). Thirty-seventh president of the U.S.A. (1969–1974), and thirty-sixth vice president in the administration of Dwight Eisenhower. Known variously as "Tricky Dick," "Mutton Face," and "Paranoid Schizophrenic," Nixon resigned from office in 1974 in the wake of the Watergate scandal, thus assuring his legacy in the form of countless other "-gate" scandals—Monicagate, Plamegate, and Ticklegate, to name just a few.

O'Reilly, William "Bill" James. Political commentator on the Fox "Fair and Balanced" News Channel, O'Reilly takes a strict moral stance on the burning issues of the day, such as whether it is appropriate to say "Happy Holidays" in lieu of "Merry Christmas." He also expresses strong views on homosexual practices. In 2004, O'Reilly was hit with a sexual harassment suit by one of his female producers. As the case was settled out of court, the rumor that Bill liked to do it wearing a Santa costume was never verified.

Reagan, Ronald Wilson (1911–2004). Once a New Deal Democrat, later a supply-side Republican; once a decrier of the Evil Empire, later the focus of numerous ethical scandals, including the Iran-Contra affair; once a B-film actor, then fortieth

* *

president of the U.S.A. Known as "the Great Communicator" for his ability to stay on message.

Rice, Condoleezza. Sixty-sixth secretary of state and former national security advisor to President G. W. Bush, Rice had a career in academia and business before joining the Bush administration. She once headed Chevron's Committee on Public Policy, and that multinational corporation honored her by naming an oil tanker after her, but controversy led to its being renamed *Altair Voyager*, which means "twelfth-brightest-star-in-the-nighttime-sky Voyager." Don't ask.

Rumsfeld, Donald. Thirteenth secretary of defense under President Ford (1975–1977), and the twenty-first secretary of defense under President G. W. Bush (2001–2006). Known as "Rummy" to his friends, and as "Rotweiller" to his detractors, Rumsfeld gave more press conferences than any previous defense Secretary. His often-repeated goal was to create a leaner army.

Santayana, George (1863–1952). Harvard philosopher and Cicero plagiarist.

Santorum, Richard "Rick" John. Former senator from Pennsylvania, Santorum is in the vanguard of right-wing Republican ideology, as demonstrated by his vigorous opposition—to abortion under any circumstances, to equal rights for homosexuals, and to removing the "theory" of intelligent design from public school curricula. However, his most memorable proposed piece of legislation, the National Weather Service Duties Act (2005), proposed prohibiting the National Weather Service from publishing weather data to the public when private-sector entities, such as AccuWeather, a company based in Santorum's home state, perform the same function commercially. In other words, you don't need to be a weatherman to know which way the money blows. (The bill was not enacted.)

Sharpton, Alfred "Al" Charles, Jr. Pentecostal minister and civil rights activist; 2004 Democratic candidate for president. Sharpton is well known for his oily hairdo, quick tongue, and firm moral pronouncements on social injustice. He is also well known for defending Tawana Brawley in a hoked-up rape case.

Stewart, Jon. Host of popular comedy show that lampoons mainstream news broadcasts. Interestingly, surveys find that his listeners are better informed about news events than listeners to mainstream news broadcasts. We live in interesting times.

Townsend, Frances Fragos. Homeland security advisor under G. W. Bush. Known as "Fraggy" among the noncommissioned officer set, Townsend is rumored to have narrowed down the whereabouts of Osama bin Laden to three of the seven continents.

Notes

i. Thanks to Gary N. Curtis at www.fallacyfiles.org for the analysis and the Lewis Carroll example.

ii. Thanks to Mardy Grothe, *Viva La Repartee* (New York: HarperCollins, 2005), for the examples.

iii. Thanks to Christopher L. Foote, senior economist at the Federal Reserve Bank of Boston, for the lead.

iv. See Carl Cannon, "Untruth and Consequences," *Atlantic*, Clinton, and Gore.

v. See Sheldon Richman, "What the Second Amendment Means," *Freedom Daily*, October 1995.

ILLUSTRATION CREDITS

—⁊⁊—

INDEX

Page numbers in italics refer to illustrations.

Adams, John, 64
ad hominem argument, 71–72
"ad homonym" argument, 71–72
affirming the consequent, 162–163, 172
after this, therefore because of this (cause and effect). *See post hoc ergo propter hoc*
Alice in Wonderland (Carroll), 162–163
Allen, Gracie, 44–45
alternate universe strategy. *See Star Trek* strategy
ambiguity, 44
See also inductive leap
analogy, weak. *See* argument from weak analogy
analytic-synthetic shuffle, 126–129
Animal Planet (television network), 170
apologizing, 97

See also guilty with explanation; *kairos* (good timing)
appeal to authority. *See argumentum ad verecundiam*
appeal to sympathy. *See argumentum ad misericordiam*
appeal to the authority of the many. *See argumentum ad populum*
argument from weak analogy, 45–50, *47*, 172
argumentum ad baculum ("argument from the stick"), 14
argumentum ad ignorantiam (argument from ignorance), 26–30, *29*
variant, 39
argumentum ad misericordiam (appeal to sympathy), 132
argumentum ad odium (argument from hatred), 25–26
argumentum ad populum (appeal to the authority of the many), 56, 58

* *

argumentum ad verecundiam (appeal to authority), 90–92, 172
Aristotle
   and the aardvark (joke), 165
   and fallacies, 14, 97, 105, 152, 163
artful equivocation, *42*, 43–45
Ashcroft, John, 117
assumption, hidden. *See* hidden assumption
Atkins, Peter, 28
Austin American-Statesman, 79
Ayer, A. J., 135

bad company technique. *See* guilt by association
Bauer, Gary, 106
Baumgartner, Jody, 114, 116
Bergman, Ingrid, 143
Boehner, John A., 78
Boortz, Neal, 45–46, 49–50
Boxer, Barbara, 39, 76–77, 175
Brady Campaign, on gun control, 157–159
Brantley, Ben, 81
Brown, Rita Mae, 109
bullshit, dazzling with. *See* tucking false premise into valid argument
bullshit, detecting, 10–17, *11*, *16*
bullshitters, selected bios of, 175–181
Burns, George, 44–45
Bush, Barbara, 100, 102, 175
Bush, George H. W., 84
   kairos (good timing), 96
Bush, George W., 144, 175
   analytic-synthetic shuffle, 126–129
   cum hoc ergo propter hoc, 106–107
   empty principles, 146–149
   false dilemma, 30–31, 33
   "God is my copilot," 84
   guilty with explanation, 92–94

inductive leap, 126
   kairos (good timing), 96, 97
butterfly effect, 119
buying conventional wisdom, 142–146

Carroll, Lewis, 48–49, 162–163
cause and effect. *See cum hoc ergo propter hoc; post hoc ergo propter hoc*
changing the subject. *See ignoratio elenchi*
Cheney, Dick, 144, 175, 176
   rhetoric of repartee, 65
   Texas sharpshooter fallacy, 20
Cheney, Lynne, 142
Chicks, Dixie. *See* Dixie Chicks
Chirac, Jacques, 176
   stacking the truth tables, 135, *136*, 138
Chorus Line, A (Broadway show), 81
Churchill, Winston, 87–88
Cicero, 122, 180
Clarke, Richard, 22–23, 26
Clinton, Bill, 73, 144
   artful equivocation, *42*, 43–44
   kairos (good timing), 96
   white lies, 139
Clinton, Hillary, 43, 73–74, 91, 144
   Food Network interview (fabricated), 167–168
   kairos (good timing), 96, 97
   MTV interview (fabricated), 170
CNN, 34, 102
Cochran, Johnnie, 154–155
coherence theory of truth, 137
Communism, McCarthy hearings on, 27, 178–179
conceptual analysis technique, 13
contextomy, 78–81, 172
conventional wisdom, 145–146
   See also buying conventional wisdom

Coolidge, Calvin, 144
Copernicus, 27
correspondence theory of truth, 137
Countdown (MSNBC), 126
CounterPunch (online newsletter), 127
cum hoc ergo propter hoc (with this,
    therefore because of this), 105–108,
    118, 119, 172

Daily Show with Jon Stewart, The. See
    Stewart, Jon
Davis, Jo Ann, 95
Deaver, Michael, 139
debate, framing the, 62–64
Declaration of Independence, 120–122
DeLay, Tom, 43, 45, 49–50, 177
denying the antecedent, 13–14,
    157–161, *160*
denying the consequent, 85
De Quincey, Thomas, 54
Deus est auriga meus. See "God is my
    charioteer"
"devil made me do it," 87
Disraeli, Benjamin, 109
distinction without a difference, 55–58,
    57
Dixie Chicks, 91, 176
doublespeak, 12
    See also tricky talk strategy
Du Bois, W. E. B., 72
Durocher, Leo, 143–144

E! (television network), 169
Earth in the Balance (Gore), 79
East Carolina University, 114
Edwards, John, 142
    E! interview (fabricated), 169
embryonic stem cell research, 146
empty principles, 146–149, *148*
epistemology, 12–13

equivocation, artful, *42*, 43–45
Esar, Evan, 109
eukairos (good timing), 97

fabrication, misleading by (authors'),
    167–170
fallacies, 12–14
    "ad homonym," 71–72
    affirming the consequent, 162–163,
        172
    analytic-synthetic shuffle, 126–129
    argument from weak analogy,
        45–50, *47*, 172
    argumentum ad ignorantiam
        (argument from ignorance),
        26–30, *29*, 39
    argumentum ad odium (argument
        from hatred), 25–26
    argumentum ad verecundiam (appeal
        to authority), 90–92, 172
    artful equivocation, *42*, 43–45
    buying conventional wisdom,
        142–146
    contextomy, 78–81, 172
    cum hoc ergo propter hoc (with this,
        therefore because of this),
        105–108, *118*, 119, 172
    denying the antecedent, 13–14,
        157–161, *160*
    distinction without a difference,
        55–58, *57*
    empty principles, 146–149, *148*
    false dilemma, 30–34, 172
    formal versus informal, 13–14
    framing the debate, 62–64
    "God is my charioteer" *(Deus est
        auriga meus)*, 82–87, *86*, 172
    guilt by association, 67–71, *68*, 172
    guilty with explanation, 92–95
    hidden assumption, 58–59

* *

ignoratio elenchi (ignorance of the issue), 22–25, *24*
improper transposition, 152–153
inductive leap, 122–126, *124*
kairos (good timing), 95–99, *99*
misleading by fabrication (authors'), 167–170
naturalistic, *60*, 61, 172
post hoc ergo propter hoc (after this, therefore because of this), 108–119, *111*, *118*
projection, 87–89
qui dicit (who says so?), 100–102
redefining truth, 132–134, *133*
reverse slippery slope, 54–55
rhetoric of repartee, 64–65
slippery slope argument, 50–54, 172
stacking the truth tables, 135–138, *136*
straw-man argument, 75–78
syllogism, 163–165
Texas sharpshooter, 19–22
tucking false premise into valid argument, 154–157
tu quoque (you too!), 72–75
unprovable premise, 120–122
weasel words, 34–41, *37*, *38*, 172
white lies, 138–142, *140*
false dilemma, fallacy of, 30–34, 172
false premise. *See* tucking false premise into valid argument; unprovable premise
Falwell, Jerry, *177*
    guilt by association, 67–69, *68*, 71
fancy footwork strategy, 105–129
    See also specific strategies
Food Network, 167–168
Ford, Robert, 73–74
formal fallacies, 12–14, 151

Fox News, 46, 142
    See also O'Reilly Factor, The
framing the debate, 62–64
Frankfurt, Harry, 12
Freakonomics (Levitt), 115–116
Freud, Sigmund, 88

gay rights, 51, 54, 55–56, 167
    and Falwell, 67–69, *68*, 177
Geffen, David, 73
genetic fallacy, 71
    See also guilt by association
Genghis Khan, 82–87, 178
Gibbs, Robert, 74
"God is my charioteer" *(Deus est auriga meus)*, 82–87, *83*, *86*, 172
Gonzales, Alberto, 97
good timing. *See kairos*
Gore, Al, 177–178
    contextomy, 79–80
    white lies, 139
Grassley, Chuck, 46, 50
Greeley, Horace, 143
Guber, Deborah Lynn, 110
guilt by association, 67–71, *68*, 172
guilty with explanation, 92–95
gun control, 157–161, *160*

Halbrook, Stephen, 158
Hamlet (Shakespeare), 165
Hannity & Colmes (Fox News), 46
Harris, Sam, 28–30
Henry, Patrick, 143
Heraclitus, 123
hidden assumption, 58–59
    See also naturalistic fallacy
Hitler, Adolf, 71, 87–89, 178
Hoekstra, Peter, 62
Holmes, Sherlock, 143
Home & Garden television, 168–169

Hurricane Katrina, 100, 102

ignoratio elenchi (ignorance of the issue), 22–25, *24*
immigrants, illegal, 163–164
improper transposition, 152–153
Imus, Don, 100
inductive leap (drawing conclusions from ambiguous evidence), 122–126, *124*
informal fallacies, 14
insanity defense, 87
Institute of International Education, 69–70
Iran and nuclear weapons, 135, *136*, 138

James, William, 137–138
Japanese American internment (World War II), apologizing for, 96
Jefferson, Thomas, 120–122, 178
Jensen, Robert, 127–128
Johndroe, Gordon, 20
Journal of Statistics Education, 110

kairos (good timing), 95–99, *99*
Kant, Immanuel, 126, 147
Katzenbach, Nicholas B., 72
Kennedy, John F., 65
Kennedy, Joseph, 65
Kennedy, Randall, 101
Kerry, John, 77–78, 90, 142, 153, 178
  argumentum ad populum, 56, 58
  distinction without a difference, 55–56
Khan, Genghis. *See* Genghis Khan
Kinkajou (of *Meerkat Manor*), 170
Kucinich, Dennis
  Home & Garden interview (fabricated), 168–169

Laird, Melvin, 125
Lakoff, George, 36
Leahy, Patrick, 65
Lee, Kahi, 168–169
Levitt, Steven, 115–116
Lewinsky, Monica, 43, 44
light's-better-here phenomenon. *See ignoratio elenchi* (ignorance of the issue)
linguistic analysis, 12
Locke, John, 121–122
logical fallacies. *See* formal fallacies
Los Angeles Times, 145
Luntz, Frank, 36

Manson, Charles, 70–71
Marx, Groucho, 85, 149
May, Michael, 145
McCarthy, Joseph, 27, 178–179
  guilt by association, 69–71
McCorvey, Norma, 39–40
McIntosh, David, 79
McMaster, H. R., 125
McNamara, Francis Terry, 125
Mearns, Hughes, 30
Menand, Louis, 143
misleading by fabrication (authors'), 167–170
missing the point. *See ignoratio elenchi* (ignorance of the issue)
Moore, G. E., 137
Morris, Jonathan, 114, 116
MTV (television network), 170
Murray, Shailagh, 162–163
Murrow, Edward R., 69

Nagin, Ray, 100, 101–102
naturalistic fallacy, *60*, 61, 172
New Yorker, 143
New York Times, The, 72, 73, 81

Nixon, Richard, 144, 179
  "ad homonym" argument, 71–72
  kairos (good timing), 97

Obama, Barack, 73–74, 144
  MTV interview (fabricated), 170
Olbermann, Keith, 126
On Murder (De Quincey), 54
O'Reilly, Bill, 179
  hidden assumption, 59–61
O'Reilly Factor, The (Fox News), 59–61
Orwell, George, 35
out-of-context quotes. *See* contextomy

Paulos, John, 109
Peirce, Charles Sanders, 137–138
personal attacks. *See* "so's your
  mother" strategy
petard, hoisting one's own, 163, 165
Philip Morris, 41
Poole, Steven, 39, 41
post hoc ergo propter hoc (after this,
  therefore because of this), 108–119,
  111, 118
Powell, Colin, 22–23
  inductive leap, 126
pragmatist theory of truth, 137–138
principles, empty, 146–149, *148*
projection, 87–89
public-record theory of truth, 138
pugio tuus est interfector tuus ("your
  own dagger is your killer"),
  164–165
Putnam, Hilary, 137

questionable premise. *See* unprovable
  premise
qui dicit (who says so?), 100–102
quod erat demonstrandum ("which was
  to be demonstrated"), 163

Ray, Rachel, 167–168
Reagan, Ronald, 139, 179–180
  redefining truth, 132–134, *133*
  redefining truth, 132–134, *133*
repartee, rhetoric of, 64–65
reverse slippery slope, 54–55
rhetorical strategies. *See* "so's your
  mother" strategy
rhetoric of repartee, 64–65
Rice, Condoleezza, 180
  straw-man argument, 76–77
Richardson, Bill
  Animal Planet interview
    (fabricated), 170
Roe v. Wade, 39–40, 115
Rolly, Paul, 164
Ross, Marcus, 134
Rove, Karl, 165
Rumsfeld, Donald, 92–94, 180
  argumentum ad ignorantiam
    (argument from ignorance),
    26–28, *29*, 30
  argumentum ad odium (argument
    from hatred), 25–26
  fallacy of false dilemma, 32
  ignoratio elenchi (ignorance of the
    issue), 22–23, *24*
Russell, Bertrand, 137

Salt Lake Tribune, 164
Santayana, George, 122–124, 180
Santorum, Rick, 180–181
  distinction without a difference, 58
  slippery slope argument, 51–52, 54
Sartre, Jean-Paul, 135
Schilling, Curt, 90, 91
September 11 terrorist attacks, 22, 26,
  31, 34, 96, 117, 177
Shadegg, John, 62
Shakespeare, William, 165

Sharpton, Al, 181
    improper transposition, 152–153
Simpson, O. J., 154–155
slavery, apologizing for, 96
slippery slope argument, 50–55, 172
Smiley, Tavis, 152–153
Smith, Al, 64
"so's your mother" strategy, 67–102
    See also specific strategies
Springsteen, Bruce, 90
stacking the truth tables, 135–138, 136
Star Trek strategy, 131–149
    See also specific strategies
statistics, and post hoc arguments,
    108–112, 111
Stewart, Jon, 12, 117, 181
    The Daily Show, 114–115, 116,
        142, 181
straw-man argument, 75–78
    See also contextomy
Supreme Court, 46, 51–52, 54
    Roe v. Wade, 39–40, 115
syllogism, 163–165
synthetic statement, 128
    See also analytic-synthetic shuffle

Teletubbies (television show). See
    Tinky Winky
Texas sharpshooter fallacy, 19–22
Think Progress (newsletter), 62
Thurmond, Strom, 117
timing, good. See kairos
Tinky Winky, 67–69, 68
Townsend, Frances Fragos, 34, 39,
    181
transposition, improper, 152–153
trash talk, 67
tricky talk strategy, 19–65
    See also specific strategies
triple-talk, 26

tucking false premise into valid
    argument, 154–157
tu quoque (you too!), 72–75

U. S. Congress, 62–63, 139
    HUAC hearings, 69–71, 179
    See also specific members
U. S. Constitution, 157–161, 160
unprovable premise, 120–122
Unspeak, 39, 41
Utah Republican Convention, 163–164

valid argument, false premise in. See
    tucking false premise into valid
    argument
Verdi, Robert, 169
Vietnam War
    and Kerry, 78, 178
    "lessons" of, and inductive leap,
        125–126
Vines, General John, 106–107

Washington Post, 109
Washington Post Radio, 162
Watergate, 97, 179
weak analogy, argument from, 45–50,
    47, 172
weasel words, 34–41, 37, 38, 172
White House, 97
    See also specific presidents
white lies, 138–142, 140
"who says so?". See qui dicit
Will, George, 109, 110–112
with this, therefore because of this
    (cause and effect). See cum hoc ergo
    propter hoc
Wolfson, Howard, 73
Wynette, Tammy, 91

Acknowledgments

—ᴡᴡ—

Above all, we are indebted to our editor, Ann Treistman, who nudged us in the direction of the topic for this book, and to our agent, Julia Lord, who magically makes things—like books—happen.

Thanks to that book designer par excellence, Brady McNamara, who once again has turned our scribblings into museum-quality art.

The usual suspects have contributed tax-free jokes: Gil Eisner; Herb Klein; our man in South Carolina, Patrick Rutledge; our man in Taiwan, Danny Bloom; plus a number of anonymous callers-in, particularly on Tom Ashbrook's *On Point* show. Thanks.

And, as always, a huge thank-you to Freke, Samara, Eloise, and Esther, who tolerated our sometimes obsessive tomfoolery with amazing grace.

Penultimately, yet with a certain sense of ultimacy, we'd like to thank the prime trio behind Image Books: Michael Jacobs, who conceived of that imprint and honored us by making us its flagship; Leslie Stoker, who so ably took care of business; and Beau Friedlander, who not only talks the talk but, yes, walks like a duck. Beau is, well, a beaut, so a big huzzah for him.

Dan would also like to thank his dog, Binx. (Don't ask.)